The
Ashes
— Miscellany —

The
Ashes
— Miscellany —

BY CLIVE BATTY

VSP

Vision Sports Publishing
19–23 High Street
Kingston upon Thames
Surrey KT1 1LL

www.visionsp.co.uk

Published by Vision Sports Publishing 2008
Reprinted 2009.
This revised and updated edition published by
Vision Sports Publishing in 2011.

ISBN 13: 978-1-907637-33-9

Printed and bound in Germany by GGP Media GmbH

Typeset by Palimpsest Book Production Limited,
Falkirk, Stirlingshire

A CIP catalogue record for this book is
available from the British Library

FOREWORD

By David Gower

Whatever else happens in the world of cricket 'The Ashes', as one of the sport's most enduring contests, remains incredibly special. The Ashes themselves, contained as they are in what must be the smallest of the world's great sporting trophies, just four and a half inches tall, rely heavily on history and symbolism for their importance, yet even if many of the players have forgotten or never knew who the Hon. Ivo Bligh, the 8th Earl of Darnley, was, the energy and pride that goes into an Ashes series is likely to be unsurpassable.

For someone from my era the ultimate challenge was to do well against the West Indies team which dominated world cricket through the Eighties and I say "do well" and not "to beat" only because the latter phrase reeked of the impossible. The West Indies had the greatest collection of stars of the era and set standards that have been matched since only by the Australians of recent years, whose teams led by Border, Taylor, Waugh and Ponting made winning a simple habit.

Yet for me there was always a special feeling about the Ashes and every time that the Australians came to England or we stepped on the plane to head Down Under there was a surge of anticipation and adrenalin. Whenever we went there you knew from the moment you got off that plane that you were in a contest. The sledging, plenty of examples of which appear in the pages that follow, would begin at immigration, continue through customs and escalate in the baggage hall. In the time it takes to get through an international airport it is amazing the number of new adjectives one can hear put alongside the word 'Pom'.

Customs, as in the officials not as in time-honoured habits, could also make life tough in other ways. Arriving at Perth one year half our team failed to spot the trap in not ticking "yes" to the question on the customs form pertaining to any wooden items we might be bringing into the country. Maybe the bowlers thought their bats just did not count for much anyway but to Customs they were the perfect excuse for an all-out search through each and every bag with the man rifling through Ian Botham's bags taking the gold medal for ultra-efficient and time-consuming investigation. Mind you, one never knew what you might find in the great man's bags and I daresay curiosity got the better of him. Nowadays all you will find therein are industrial quantities of golf balls!

All this of course paled into insignificance compared to the battles on the field. Undoubtedly the proudest moments of my career came in Ashes contests and some of the ones I would most prefer to forget too. Take for instance the series of 1985 and 1989. In the former I was able to lead the victorious team by example, with runs aplenty, and there is no better feeling, at least not on a cricket pitch, than to have been so fully involved in an Ashes triumph. Four years later it was time for Allan Border to gain his revenge and it left me plumbing some very uncomfortable depths.

As such it is much more fun to look back on that '85 series and pick out those moments that define a series, those little bits of magic and luck that make all the difference. At Lord's we dropped Allan Border on his way to 196. Mike Gatting, of course a winning captain himself in 1986/7, caught him at short leg, tried to throw the ball up and let it slip. Australia won the Test and it was 1–1. Three matches later at Edgbaston we went ahead and it took a hotly disputed decision to get us on track on the final afternoon. Wayne Phillips hit one onto Allan Lamb's instep at silly point, from where the ball looped to me at silly mid-off. I can swear I saw it all the way – I must have been looking to see the rebound! – and the umpires concurred. 2–1. On the first day of the final Test at The Oval Graham Gooch and I both scored centuries and by the fourth day we had won the match and the series and I was up on the balcony holding the urn. It always struck me as an irony though that at the moment of such success I was holding aloft something which most of the crowd below probably could not even see. At least if you win the FA Cup you need two hands to lift the trophy. With the Ashes the thumb and forefinger will do. But does it matter? Does it heck! Even so I have always said there was something Monty Pythonesque about it all, like a scene from *The Life of Brian*, without the religious connotations, of course.

That was my personal highlight but there were many other Ashes moments to savour. I was there, as Max Boyce might say, for Botham's Ashes, an incredible series and not just for the legendary comeback at Headingley. I was there for the 86/7 Gatting tour when Martin Johnson wrote of the team just before the First Test in Brisbane, "There are only three things this side cannot do. They cannot bat. They cannot bowl. They cannot field." To win the Test series, the one-day championship and the Perth Challenge in between was no mean feat in that case!

I played against some of the true greats; early on I came up against the Chappells, Lillee, Thomson and Marsh. Allan Border emerged as one of the gutsiest and most prolific batsmen of all time. There are many others, too numerous to mention, whose performances epitomised the challenge of the Ashes. Sadly I never got to play against Shane Warne; it would have been great just to have faced him, better still to maybe have got the better of him. On the other hand he might have seen me off as easily as many of the others who made up his 708 Test wickets.

In many ways Warne himself is the perfect example of what the Ashes mean to all those who have ever played in even one Test between England and Australia. The man was voted cricketer of the century by Wisden and enthralled cricket lovers around the world, yet his finest hours all seemed to be in Ashes series; the Gatting wonder ball at Old Trafford that announced Warne's arrival, the hat trick in Melbourne, through to his pre-eminence during the 5–0 trouncing of the old foe in 2006/07 took him into retirement with a huge smile all over his face.

He is of course included in this book as an Ashes Legend, something of an understatement. There is much more besides, a host of other fascinating facts and figures on the Ashes to date. With the series of 2013 approaching it will not be long before there are a few more tales to add.

David Gower

— ENGLAND V AUSTRALIA:
ALL-TIME TEST RESULTS —

Australia hold a clear lead in Test match victories over England in matches played between the sides since 1877. The Aussies have won more than half of all their home encounters, and can also claim a narrow advantage in Tests played in England. The full stats for Test match results between the two nations currently read:

	Played	England wins	Australia wins	Draws
In England	156	45	47	64
In Australia	170	57	86	27
Total	326	102	133	91

— THE FIRST ENGLAND-AUSTRALIA MATCH —

Although it wasn't called a Test match (the term didn't pass into general usage until 1884 when it appeared in the *Melbourne Argus*) the first meeting between England and Australia took place in Melbourne in March 1877.

England's party was led by James Lillywhite, a 35-year-old left-arm bowler with Sussex who was also the tour manager and promoter. Many of the 12 players who made the trip on the *SS Poonah*, which sailed from Southampton on 23 September 1876, were not first-choices – a number of leading names, including WG Grace, were absent having been unimpressed by Lillywhite's offer of £200 per man for a six-month tour that included 48-day boat trips at either end. As a result of these absentees, the tourists' batting line up was considered to be weaker than the bowling, which featured three well-known players in Alfred Shaw, Allen Hill and 49-year-old James Southerton.

The tour didn't have the best of starts. After a number of warm-up matches in Australia, the party travelled to New Zealand where wicketkeeper Ted Pooley of Surrey got into a fight with a local man who had refused to pay a gambling debt, and was promptly arrested. Although he was found not guilty of any offence in his trial at the Supreme Court, the incident ended his active participation in the tour and he never appeared in Test cricket.

Down to 11 players, Lillywhite's men returned to Australia the day before facing a local team drawn from just two associations, New South Wales and Victoria, and captained by Dave Gregory. Contemporary reference books would later describe the match as a combined Melbourne and Sydney XI v James Lillywhite's Professional Touring team, but the press on both sides of the world were agreed that, to all intents and purposes, it was Australia v England.

At 1.05pm on 15 March 1877 Australian opener Charles Bannerman faced the first ball in Test cricket, bowled by Notts pro Alfred Shaw. No runs were scored from that opening delivery, but Bannerman got off the mark from the second ball and went on to score the first century in Test cricket, hitting 165 off 330 balls out of Australia's total of 245 before retiring hurt (see *The First Centurions*, page 40).

In reply, England were all out for 196, with Billy Midwinter (who, in a strange twist of fate, would later play for England against Australia) taking 5–78. The bowlers continued to dominate in Australia's second innings, the home side being bowled out for 104 so leaving England a highly achievable target of 153 to win. Again, though, the weaknesses in the tourists' batting were exposed, wickets fell at regular intervals and England eventually lost by 45 runs. After the match each player received a commemorative gold medal from the Victorian Cricket Association.

Lillywhite's men got their revenge in the Second Test, which was also held in Melbourne. Having taken a commanding first innings lead, England eventually won by four wickets to tie the two-match series.

First series scores:

First Test, Melbourne, March 15–19
Australia 245 & 104, England 196 & 108
Australia won by 45 runs

Second Test, Melbourne, March 31–April 4
Australia 122 & 259, England 261 & 122–6
England won by four wickets

The teams:

Australia	England
1. Charles Bannerman	1. Harry Jupp (Surrey)
2. Nathaniel Thomson	2. John Selby (Notts)
3. Tom Horan	3. Henry Charlwood (Sussex)
4. Dave Gregory (capt)	4. George Ulyett (Yorkshire)
5. Bransby Cooper	5. Andrew Greenwood (Yorkshire)
6. Billy Midwinter	6. Tom Armitage (Yorkshire)
7. Ned Gregory	7. Alfred Shaw (Notts)
8. Jack Blackham	8. Tom Emmett (Yorkshire)
9. Tom Garrett	9. Allen Hill (Yorkshire)
10. Tom Kendall	10. James Lillywhite (Sussex, capt)
11. John Hodges	11. James Southerton (Surrey)

— GOOCHIE'S DEBUT PAIR —

Future England captain Graham Gooch endured a miserable Test debut against Australia at Edgbaston in 1975, making a pair. In the first innings Gooch was caught behind by Aussie wicketkeeper Rodney Marsh and, with the pressure on him in the second innings, succumbed to another Marsh catch. After trudging back forlornly to the dressing room, Gooch's mood could only have worsened on learning that he was the first batsman to bag a pair on his Test debut since WG Grace's brother, Fred, suffered the same fate against the Aussies at The Oval in 1880.

To cheer Goochie up a bit, here's a team of players who also didn't bother the scorers on their Test debut in an Ashes match – even if, unlike the Essex batsman, they eventually managed to get off the mark in their second innings:

1. Mike Atherton (Eng), Trent Bridge, 1989
2. Victor Trumper (Aus), Trent Bridge, 1899
3. Phil Carlson (Aus), Adelaide, 1979
4. Keith Fletcher (Eng), Headingley, 1968
5. Jack Richards (Eng), Brisbane, 1986
6. Terry Jenner (Aus), Brisbane, 1970
7. Mike Smith (Eng), Headingley, 1997
8. Fred Spofforth (Aus), Melbourne, 1877
9. Dean Hedley (Eng), Old Trafford, 1997
10. Bob Massie (Aus), Lord's, 1972
11. Simon O'Donnell (Aus), Headingley, 1985

In addition to making a duck on his Test debut at Headingley in 1968, Fletcher also dropped three slip catches which the Yorkshire crowd were convinced would have been taken by local hero Phil Sharpe who was called into the Test squad but not included in the final line-up. Despite playing for England for another 14 years, Fletcher never managed to win over the Headingley public after his dismal debut.

— WICKET FIRST BALL —

It's every bowler's dream to take a wicket with his first delivery in Test cricket, but the dream only rarely becomes a reality. In fact, just three bowlers have pulled off this feat in Ashes cricket, and they are:

Bowler	Year	Venue	Batsman
Arthur Conigham (Aus)	1894	Melbourne	Archie MacLaren
Bill Bradley (Eng)	1899	Old Trafford	Frank Laver
Ted Arnold (Eng)	1903	Sydney	Victor Trumper

— ASHES LEGENDS: WG GRACE —

The first superstar of English cricket, WG Grace was already a household name when he made his Test debut against Australia at The Oval in 1880. Aged 32, he was probably past his peak but nonetheless delighted the crowd by scoring 152 – the first time an English batsman had registered a ton against the Aussies. Over the next 19 years, he played in a further 21 Tests against Australia, but only added one further century – 170 made out of 216 while he was at the crease at The Oval in 1886.

Six foot two, powerfully built with an unfeasibly long beard, Grace had an outsized personality to match his towering frame. In one charity match he insisted on batting with a broomstick but still managed to score 35 runs, the second highest score of the day. On another occasion he refused to leave the pitch when he was clean bowled first ball, exclaiming, "They came to see me bat, not to see you umpire!" He was also known for having a fierce temper, once punching a spectator at Northampton who had been shouting abuse from the stands.

He took his unconventional approach into Test cricket, filling in behind the stumps in the 1884 Oval Test against Australia when wicketkeeper Alfred Lyttleton tried his arm at bowling. Even in this cameo role, Grace was a success, dismissing Aussie batsman Billy Midwinter first ball with a leg-side catch – assisted, perhaps, by the fact that he wasn't wearing pads.

Although nominally an amateur, Grace earned more money from cricket than from practicing his profession as a doctor. England team-mate Arthur Shrewsbury suggested in his correspondence that the cost of taking Grace, along with wife and family, on the 1891/92 tour was about £3,000 (equivalent to considerably more than £100,000 today) and that Grace would drink enough wine to float a ship. His money-grabbing attitude did not endear Grace to his team-mates, while he was not universally popular in Australia either. For instance, *The Bulletin*, a Sydney publication, once memorably described him as 'burly and surly'.

After scoring more than 54,000 first-class runs in 44 seasons, Grace finally retired from cricket in his late fifties. He died from a brain haemorrhage, aged 67, at his home in Kent.

WG Grace factfile
Born: Bristol, 18 July 1848   **Died:** 23 October 1915
County: Gloucestershire
Ashes Tests: 22 (1880–99)
Batting: 1,098 runs (ave 32.29)
Bowling: 9 wickets (ave 26.22)

Others on WG Grace

"He seems different from all other cricketers – a king apart."
Fred 'The Demon' Spofforth, Australian bowler and Ashes opponent

"He was ever ready with an encouraging word for the novice, and a compassionate one for the man who made a mistake."
Lord Harris, England captain at the time of Grace's Test debut

The most famous beard in the history of sport

— JOBBING XI —

Here's a team of Ashes players whose surnames suggest they could easily have found alternative employment after their cricket careers came to an end:

1. Michael Slater (Aus, 1993–2001)
2. Mark Butcher (Eng, 1997–2003)
3. Barry Knight (Eng, 1962–68)
4. Bransby Cooper (Aus, 1877)
5. Ron Archer (Aus, 1953–56)
6. Roland Pope (Aus, 1885)
7. Jack Mason (Eng, 1897–98)
8. Geoff Miller (Eng, 1977–83)
9. Bert Ironmonger (Aus,1928–33)
10. Nick Cook (Eng, 1989)
11. Joe Hunter (Eng, 1884–85)

— THE START OF 'THE ASHES' —

The term 'The Ashes' was not coined until 1882, five years after the first series between England and Australia.

Led by Billy Murdoch, Australia were making their second visit to England, their tour including a single Test at The Oval. The match, played on a difficult pitch, was a low-scoring affair, England requiring just 85 runs to win after bowling Australia out for 122 in their second innings. The task appeared well within the reach of England, especially while opener WG Grace was going well at 51–2, but Australia refused to give up hope. In particular, fast bowler Fred 'The Demon' Spofforth was an inspiration to his team-mates, first declaring, "This thing can be done!" and then firing off a seven-wicket salvo to reduce England to 75–9. When the final batsman, Ted Peate, came to the wicket, England needed 10 runs to win. In a nerve-jangling finale, Peate was bowled by Harry Boyle, who had earlier taken the vital wicket of Grace for 32, to give Australia their first victory on English soil.

The crowd, astonished by England's dramatic collapse, initially fell silent before sportingly applauding the victors. England's unexpected defeat was much discussed in the following day's newspapers and, a few days later on 2 September 1882, a mock obituary, written by a young journalist called Reginald Brooks, appeared in *The Sporting Times*. It read:

In affectionate remembrance of English cricket which died at The Oval, 29th August, 1882. Deeply lamented by a large circle of sorrowing friends and acquaintances, R.I.P.
N.B. The body will be cremated and the Ashes taken to Australia.

The words struck a chord with the public and when, a fortnight later, England captain the Honourable Ivo Bligh set sail with his team for that winter's tour of Australia, he declared that his aim was to 'bring back the Ashes'. On his arrival in Melbourne two months later, Bligh made a similar announcement, bewildering the vast majority of Australians who had had never heard of *The Sporting Times*, let alone read it. Once explained, though, the concept of 'the Ashes' was readily embraced Down Under and soon became part of the language of the tour.

The three-match series was closely fought and attracted huge crowds, totalling more than 150,000. Indeed, the encounters were so popular that a fourth one-off game, won by Australia, was added to the tour itinerary. By then, however, England had already won the series proper 2–1, clinching 'the Ashes' with victory by 69 runs in Sydney.

Following England's victory, Bligh was presented with a small terracotta urn filled with ashes by a group of Melbourne ladies. "What better way than to actually present the English captain with the very object – albeit mythical – he had come to Australia to retrieve?" suggested one of the ladies, a Mrs Ann Fletcher. The ashes inside the urn are often said to be from one of the bails used in the decisive Sydney Test, but other theories suggest they may originate from a burnt cricket ball or, perhaps more plausibly, from a veil worn by one of Mrs Fletcher's friends.

Whatever the truth, the urn and the ashes inside it had come to symbolize the prize at stake when England and Australia played each other at cricket. In the future, with the exception of one-off clashes such as the Centenary Tests of 1977 and 1980, all meetings between the two sides would be known throughout the world as 'The Ashes'.

— ASHES VENUES: ENGLAND (AND WALES)—

The first ever Test match between England and Australia to be played in England was staged at The Oval in 1880, England winning by five wickets. Since then another seven grounds have hosted Ashes Tests, although Bramall Lane's debut in 1902 also proved to be the last time this venue was used for an England-Australia clash.

Of these eight venues, The Oval has been the luckiest for England, the home side having enjoyed 16 wins in south London. Despite its status as the home of English cricket, Lord's has been a favourite stamping ground for the visitors, the Aussies having lost just one match there since 1896! (See *Bogey Ground*, page 123)

Ground	Ashes debut	Ashes Tests	England wins	Australia wins	Draws
The Oval	1880	35	16	6	13
Old Trafford	1884	28	7	7	14
Lord's	1884	34	6	14	14
Trent Bridge	1899	20	4	7	9
Headingley	1899	24	7	9	8
Edgbaston	1902	13	5	3	5
Bramall Lane	1902	1	0	1	0
Sophia Gardens	2009	1	0	1	0

In 2009 Sophia Gardens in Cardiff became the first ground outside England or Australia to host an Ashes match, and the Welsh public were treated to as a thriller as England's last-wicket pair of Jimmy Anderson and Monty Panesar hung on for a nerve-jangling draw.

— IN THE COMMENTARY BOX —

Numerous Ashes cricketers have made the transition from player to commentator, some more seamlessly than others. Among the former England and Australian stars currently earning their living by pontificating on the game, either on TV or the radio, are these illustrious names:

Jonathan Agnew (Eng, Test Match Special)
Paul Allott (Eng, Sky Sports)
Mike Atherton (Eng, Sky Sports)
Richie Benaud (Aus, Channel Nine)
Ian Botham (Eng, Sky Sports)
Geoff Boycott (Eng, Test Match Special)
Ian Chappell (Aus, Channel Nine)
Angus Fraser (Eng, Test Match Special)
David Gower (Eng, Sky Sports)
Tony Greig (Eng, Channel Nine)
Ian Healy (Aus, Channel Nine)
Nasser Hussain (Eng, Sky Sports)
Alec Stewart (Eng, Test Match Special)
Phil Tufnell (Eng, Test Match Special)

David Lloyd (Eng, Sky Sports)
Mark Taylor (Aus, Channel Nine)
Michael Vaughan (Eng, Test Match Special)
Bob Willis (Eng, Sky Sports)

— BEERS BY THE DOZEN —

It has become something of a tradition for the Australian touring party to get stuck into a few cans of beer – or 'tinnies' as the Aussies call them – on their occasional flights over to England for an Ashes series.

For many years, Doug Walters held the record for the most beers consumed between Sydney and London but, in 1985, Rodney Marsh set a new standard by downing 45 cans. However, as Dennis Lillee later recalled, Marsh required a little bit of help from his team-mates as he continued on his record-breaking attempt: "I acted as pacemaker on the first leg – from Melbourne to Honolulu – then others helped out on the last two stretches as I enjoyed a good sleep. When we got to London, Graeme Wood and I were fresh enough to help him off the plane. The man needed some help after 45 cans!"

Marsh's record stood for just four years before it was smashed by David Boon, who knocked back 52 beers on the flight preceding the 1989 Ashes series. Understandably, perhaps, Boon was a little worse for wear when the plane arrived in London but he recovered to make a significant contribution to Australia's crushing 4-0 victory, averaging 55.25 across the series.

— SHANE'S LONG ROOM TRIBUTE —

Of all the many awards and accolades Shane Warne has received, perhaps the most satisfying came in 2005 when he became only the fourth Australian cricketer (after Victor Trumper, Don Bradman and Keith Miller) to have his portrait hung in the Long Room at Lord's, the inner sanctum of the home of English cricket.

The Aussie spin bowler's likeness was captured by London artist Fanny Rush over a number of sittings at her Chelsea studio during the momentous 2005 Ashes series, Warne's last in England before he retired from international cricket two years later. The portrait that emerged from these sessions shows a smiling Warne, flicking the ball in the air before preparing to bowl one of his devillish deliveries. "From the moment I heard that MCC wanted to commission me to paint Shane Warne, a very strong image of how to portray him floated into my mind," the artist later explained. "I knew his reputation as a fearsome bowler, and I envisaged him in the portrait as if seen from a batsman's point of view, bearing down formidably and with supreme confidence. Over the months that it took to complete the painting, I got to know him as a person, too; he is a delightful man, and I feel that I have also caught this aspect of him in the portrait."

— THE ASHES URN: ESSENTIAL FACTS —

- The original urn, presented to England captain Ivo Bligh (later Lord Darnley) by a group of cricket-loving Melbourne ladies in 1883, is made of terracotta and is just four inches high.
- The urn was presented to the MCC in 1927 following Bligh's death by his widow, Lady Darnley, who, back in the days when she was plain old Florence Morphy, had been one of the Melbourne ladies who gave the artefact to Bligh. The pair married in 1884, one year after meeting during England's tour of Australia.
- Winning Ashes teams are not presented with the urn, which is simply too fragile to be used as a conventional trophy. During the domination of the Ashes by Australia in the 1990s some Aussies argued that the urn should be handed over to Mark Taylor's all-conquering side. The MCC ignored these demands and, instead, commissioned a large-scale replica trophy in Waterford Crystal to be awarded to the victors. It was first presented to a triumphant Taylor after the Ashes series of 1998/99.
- Previously, in 1948, a ten-inch replica of the urn was presented to Don Bradman's 'Invincibles' after their crushing 4–0 victory in England. The replica is currently on show at Cricket Australia's offices near the Melbourne Cricket Ground.
- Much to the annoyance of many Aussies, the famous urn has only returned Down Under twice. The first occasion was in 1988 for a museum tour to coincide with Australia's Bicentennial celebrations. More recently, the urn accompanied the England side on their 2006/07 tour of Australia, making a final appearance at the Tasmanian Museum Art Gallery on 21 January 2007.
- The urn, along with the red and gold velvet bag in which it was originally wrapped and the scorecard from the 1882 Oval Test which gave rise to the Ashes legend, can be seen in the MCC Cricket Museum at Lord's. In 2003 the urn was removed from the museum and taken to a specialist restorer for repairs. Following an X-ray examination, the main problem was identified as the degeneration of an adhesive used to repair the urn some 75 years earlier.

— ONE-OFF NIGHTMARES —

Of the dozens of cricketers who featured in just one Ashes Test, quite a few endured eminently forgettable debuts. Perhaps the most famous case is that of Fred Tate, a 35-year-old off-spinner with Sussex who was called up for the Fourth Test at Old Trafford in 1902 – a match England had to win to have any chance of regaining the Ashes.

Tate failed to take a wicket in Australia's first innings before contributing five not out batting at number eleven. He did manage to take two wickets in the visitors' second innings, but crucially he also dropped a simple catch which allowed Aussie captain Joe Darling to top score with 37. Tate was given a chance to redeem himself when he went out to bat a second time, the scoreboard showing England on 116–9 and requiring just eight runs to win. A huge roar went up from the crowd as Tate snicked a streaky four, but two balls later he was bowled by Jack Saunders' shooter. To add to Tate's misery, the home crowd roundly booed him as he made his way back to the pavilion.

"I've a little lad at home who'll make up for this," said a distraught Tate after England's three-run defeat. Remarkably, his prediction proved correct as his seven-year-old son, Maurice Tate, developed into one of England's best ever fast-medium bowlers.

Meanwhile, other players whose only Ashes appearance did not exactly go to plan include:

- **Alexander Webbe (Eng):** An amateur who was a member of Lord Harris's tour of Australia in 1879, Webbe took two catches on his Test debut in Melbourne in 1879. His batting was less impressive, however, and scores of 4 and 0 contributed to England's crushing defeat by ten wickets.
- **Fred Grace (Eng):** Played alongside his brothers, the famous WG and the less well known Edward Grace, in the 1880 Test at The Oval, but failed to shine, collecting a pair. Within a month he was dead from pneumonia, one theory being that the illness developed from a chill he caught while fielding in his only international appearance.
- **William Robertson (Aus):** 'Digger' Robertson's sole Test in Melbourne in 1885 was less than glorious, the right-hand batsman contributing just two runs to his side's cause in two completed innings and taking 0–24 with his legbreaks.
- **Walter Mead (Eng):** Lord's has rarely been a happy hunting ground for England against Australia, and the 1899 match between the sides didn't buck the trend. One of the reasons for England's ten-wicket defeat was the poor showing of debut boy Mead who scored just seven runs and conceded 91 while taking a solitary wicket.
- **Roy Park (Aus):** A qualified doctor, Park was called out on medical duties the night before his Test debut against England at Melbourne in 1920. The lack of sleep clearly affected his performance, as he was clean bowled for a first-ball duck. His wife, sitting in the stands, is said to have missed the one ball her husband faced in Test cricket as she was bending down to pick up her knitting. Park did just as poorly with the ball, bowling a single expensive over of off-spin before being hurriedly withdrawn from the Australian attack.

- **Arthur Dolphin (Eng):** The gloriously named Dolphin, a wicketkeeper with Yorkshire, failed to make the most of his one international call-up against the Aussies at Melbourne in 1921. Although he held on to one catch, Dolphin made just a single run in his two innings as England went down to an emphatic eight-wicket defeat.
- **Ray Robinson (Aus):** Middle-order batsman Robinson made just three runs in his first Test innings against England at Brisbane in 1936. Second time round he fared even worse, scoring only two runs as Australia were dismissed for 58 to lose by a humiliating 322-run margin.
- **Arnie Sidebottom (Eng):** A gifted all-round sportsman who played football for Manchester United, Huddersfield and Halifax, Sidebottom was called up for his only Test against Australia at Trent Bridge in 1985. After scoring just two runs, he took 1–65 before leaving the field injured. Maybe he should have stuck to soccer. His son, Ryan, played 22 Tests for England between 2001–10.
- **Mike Smith (Eng):** The Gloucestershire swing bowler followed a first innings duck at Headingley in 1997 with a paltry four runs second time round, and he had even less luck with the ball. After seeing Graham Thorpe drop a simple slip catch, Smith finished with unimpressive figures of 0–89 as the Aussies piled on the runs, declaring on 501–9. Smith's only Test ended in defeat, England going down by an innings and 61 runs.

— JUST SIX BOWLERS REQUIRED —

In a low-scoring Ashes encounter at Old Trafford in 1888 the England and Australia captains called on just three bowlers apiece to set a record for the fewest bowlers to be used in a Test match.

The Aussie trio of John Ferris, Charlie Turner and Sammy Woods restricted England to 172 on the first day, but on a sticky wicket it surprisingly proved to be a more than adequate total. England left-arm spinner Bobby Peel made the most of the favourable conditions, taking 11–68 in the match and, supported by fellow spinner Johnny Briggs and medium pacer George Lohmann, was instrumental in his side's triumph by an innings and 21 runs – a result which gave England a 2–1 victory in the three-Test series.

— COOK'S TASTY DISHES —

Those pundits who were querying Alastair Cook's place in the England side prior to the 2010/11 Ashes series were made to look pretty silly by the end of the tour. The opening batsman's brilliant displays, which included a superb unbeaten double century in the First Test at Brisbane and big tons at Adelaide and Sydney, were a key factor in the tourists' eventual 3–1 series win.

Here, for stat fans especially, are the full details of Cook's mostly magnificent innings Down Under:

Test	Venue	Score	Minutes	Balls	4s	6s
First	Brisbane	67	283	168	6	-
		235*	625	428	26	-
Second	Adelaide	148	428	269	18	-
Third	Perth	32	91	63	3	1
		13	24	16	1	-
Fourth	Melbourne	82	212	152	11	-
Fifth	Sydney	189	488	342	16	-
Totals		766	2151	1438	81	1

*not out

Cook carries his bat in Brisbane.

— RICHIE'S TOP TEN —

In 2006 veteran cricket commentator Richie Benaud was invited by leading Australian newspaper *The Age* to select his top ten Ashes moments of all time. In chronological order, these were his choices:

1. **England beaten at home by Australia for the first time, 1882**
   -"There were many heroes: Fred Spofforth for his bowling and his rallying call, Billy Murdoch for his captaincy and Hugh Massie for his brilliant 55 out of the first 66 second-innings runs."

2. **Bodyline, 1932/33**
   -"Perfectly legal under the laws of cricket as they stood at the time. Bradman's batting average was halved, England won the series and relations between England and Australia were sorely tested in those early Depression years."

3. **Australia's fightback, 1936/37**
   -"It is the only occasion a team has won a five-match series after being two down."

4. **Headingley, 1948**
   -"No batting side had ever made over 400 in the fourth innings of a Test to win. Australia managed it here with Arthur Morris making 182 and Bradman 173 not out."

5. **Jim Laker's 19 wickets at Old Trafford, 1956**
   -"It was one of the most sensational bowling performances of all time."

6. **Old Trafford, 1961**
   -"Australia came from the clouds to win on the last afternoon and retain the Ashes."

7. **Lord's, 1972**
   -"This was Bob Massie's match; he took 16 wickets in his Test debut on a green Lord's pitch."

8. **Shane Warne's 'ball of the century', 1993**
   -"Other batsmen, and Mike Gatting's nearest and dearest, thought of it as the ball from hell. Leg spinners muse over it as the ball from heaven."

9. **Steve Waugh's two hundreds at Old Trafford, 1997**
   -"Steve Waugh made 116 and 108 and Australia won with half a day to spare."

10. **Edgbaston, 2005**
    -"The closest margin for victory in an Ashes Test. Such was the excitement that, on the fourth morning, which might have lasted two balls, the gates were closed an hour before the start."

— ASHES LEGENDS: FRED SPOFFORTH —

Fred Spofforth was the first in a long line of Australian quicks to have terrorised English batsmen in Ashes matches, earning the nickname 'The Demon' from the British media for his fast and accurate bowling.

Spofforth made his Test debut against England in the second Melbourne Test of 1877, having refused to play in the inaugural match between the countries when his preferred choice as wicketkeeper, Billy Murdoch, was not selected. Varying his bowling to great effect – Spofforth's repertoire included a yorker, a top-spinner and a zipping break-back from the offside – he took four wickets on his debut, despite finishing on the losing side.

Two years later, Spofforth became the first bowler to claim a Test hat-trick, achieving the feat while taking 13 wickets in the Sydney Test of 1879. Yet he surpassed even this impressive achievement in the Oval Test of 1882, striking 14 times as Australia won a nerve-wracking match – the one, incidentally, which gave rise to the Ashes legend – by just seven runs.

'Demon bowling'

As well as being a fine bowler, Spofforth was also an extremely aggressive one. His party piece was to unsettle an incoming batsman by glaring at him, as one nineteenth-century cricketer recalled: "His look went through me like a red-hot poker. Halfway down the wicket something made me turn round and look at him over my shoulder. And there he was, still fixing me with his eye."

Spofforth played his last Test against England in January 1887. After finishing his career at the age of 34, he left for England to get married and became managing director of the Star Tea Company, which was owned by his father-in-law. In 1996, 70 years after his death, he was one of the first ten cricketers to be inducted into the Australian Cricket Hall of Fame.

Fred Spofforth factfile
Born: Sydney, 9 September 1853   **Died:** 4 June 1926
State: New South Wales, Victoria
Ashes Tests: 18 (1877–87)
Batting: 217 runs (ave 9.43)
Bowling: 94 wickets (ave 18.41)

Others on Spofforth
"One of the best bowlers ever seen."
Lord Harris, England captain between 1878 and 1884

"I knew he'd do it. He's too much for me."
England batsman **'Monkey' Hornby** after being dismissed by Spofforth

— DOMINANT ERAS —

The most number of Tests played during which one side has continuously held the Ashes:

Team	Years	Tests
Australia	1989–2005	44
Australia	1958/59–1971	32
Australia	1934–53	29
England	1882/83–1891/92	21
Australia	1897/98–1903/04	20

At the other end of the scale, England held the Ashes for just 15 months after their 2005 triumph before Australia's 2006/07 series win was confirmed by victory in the Third Test at Perth.

— THROUGH THE GATE —

Attendance figures and receipts for the five Ashes Tests of 2005:

Test	Venue	Attendance	Receipts
First Test	Lord's	88,638	£3,612,724
Second Test	Edgbaston	81,870	£2,970,226
Third Test	Old Trafford	111,657	£2,480,000
Fourth Test	Trent Bridge	65,583	£1,746,786
Fifth Test	The Oval	106,790	£2,824,556

— GOWER TURNS BIGGLES —

An elegant left-hander, David Gower was England's most successful batsman against the Aussies during the 1980s. He particularly enjoyed the 1985 series, when he scored a record number of runs for an Englishman in a home Ashes series, 732, at an impressive average of 81.33.

However, in addition to his batting achievements, Gower will also be remembered for a bizarre incident on the 1990/91 Ashes tour. Already 2–0 down to the Australians, England were playing against Queensland in Carrara when Gower and fellow batsman John Morris left the ground to be taken up in a pair of pre-war Tiger Moths. Not content with the standard tourist flight, Gower and Morris encouraged their pilots to fly low over the stadium while the England pair at the crease, Allan Lamb and Robin Smith, looked on in astonishment.

When they got wind of the stunt the England management team, led by captain Graham Gooch, were distinctly unamused. Despite England's ten-wicket victory in the match, the two high-flying players were fined £1,000 each. It seems likely, too, that the black mark incurred by the 'Biggles' episode was never really erased. Morris failed to add to his three England caps while Gower, arguably the most gifted English batsman of his generation, only played a handful more times for his country.

— JIMMY AND MONTY SAVE ENGLAND —

In the First Test of the 2009 Ashes series in Cardiff, Australia looked almost certain winners when England's last-wicket pair of Jimmy Anderson and Monty Panesar came together with over an hour's play remaining. However, against all the odds, the duo bravely resisted everything the Baggy Greens could throw at them, bringing the prospect of an unlikely draw tantalisingly closer with every blocked delivery.

As the nation willed the pair on, here's how Tom Bellwood reported the closing minutes of the match is his over-by-over coverage on the *Daily Mail* website:

18.20: I feel sick with nerves. Don't know what they are feeling out there. Monty nicks a single and there's more dogged defence from Anderson. Another over slides by. 245–9.

ENGLAND NEED TO BAT UNTIL 6.40pm TO DRAW THIS TEST.

18.25: Huge shout from Siddle – he appeals for about an hour – but it is sliding down leg. Siddle looks furious. A short ball gets Panesar to duck nicely out of the way and leaves another couple. 245–9.

18.28: The pressure here is excruciating. Heroic stuff from Anderson and Panesar. So much to ask from this pair as they nick a single down to third man to leave us ten minutes away from a hard fought draw. Come on, lads!! 246–9.

18.32: Marcus North into Panesar. Panesar hits him for four after a misfield!

ENGLAND LEAD BY 12!

I think we're there. Every ball that gets fended off is greeted with huge cheers. 251–9.

18.36: The 12th man Shafayat is on with gloves and drinks and Ponting is incensed at the perceived time wasting. Who cares. I've never been so glad to see a maiden over. 251–9.

18.39: We'll have one more over before we safely call it a draw. Strauss looks agonisingly on at the action.

18.42: IT'S A DRAW! PANESAR AND ANDERSON – HEROES!

— THE GREAT ASHES SERIES: 'BODYLINE', AUSTRALIA 1932/33 —

Known as the 'Bodyline' series, England's 1932/33 tour of Australia was the most controversial in Ashes history. Indeed, relations between the two countries deteriorated so badly that at one point it seemed the series would be abandoned.

Two figures, one on each side, were at the centre of the drama: England captain Douglas Jardine, and Australian batsman Don Bradman. The latter's domination of the England bowlers had largely been responsible for Australia's Ashes victory in 1930, and Jardine was determined to prevent a repeat. After discussions with his two main fast bowlers, Harold Larwood and Bill Voce, Jardine devised an anti-

Bradman strategy which he termed 'leg theory', but which soon became known as 'Bodyline'. Essentially, this involved the bowling of short-pitched deliveries aimed at the batsman's body, supported by a strong leg-side field. The theory was that any batsman using his bat to protect himself against a bouncer would run the risk of being caught in the leg trap.

In the First Test at Sydney the plan worked a treat. Stan McCabe, with an unbeaten 187, was the only Australian batsman to successfully adapt his game to 'Bodyline' and England took a big first innings lead thanks to centuries by Herbert Sutcliffe, Wally Hammond and, on his Test debut, the Nawab of Pataudi. In their second innings, the Australians were skittled out for just 164, Larwood taking 5–28 in a ferocious spell, and England won easily by ten wickets.

The Second Test at Melbourne was a low-scoring affair, due to a stodgy wicket. Requiring just 251 to win, England were strong favourites but collapsed to 139 all out. Australian spinner Bill 'Tiger' O'Reilly was his side's matchwinner with five wickets in the innings and ten in the match.

England's 'Bodyline' strategy had already produced some grumblings from the Aussies, but at Adelaide in the Third Test the simmering tensions between the two teams erupted into outright confrontation. After England had posted a reasonable score of 341 in their first innings, Larwood tore into the Australian batting. First, he struck the Australian captain, Bill Woodfall, a painful blow just above the heart; then, later in the innings, he fractured Bert Oldfield's skull with a bouncer that deflected off the Aussie wicketkeeper's bat. "This isn't cricket, it's war," an irate Woodfall advised England's tour manager, Pelham Warner. The Australian Board of Control was equally incensed, sending an official complaint to the MCC after Australia's 338-run defeat in which it objected to England's 'unsportsmanlike' approach. Meanwhile, the home fans made their feelings felt by jeering the two main 'Bodyline' protagonists, Jardine and Larwood. There were also reports of Union flags being burned in the streets around the ground.

For a few days, it appeared that the remainder of the tour might be cancelled. Jardine strongly objected to the accusation that England's play had been 'unsportsmanlike', and insisted that unless the term was withdrawn he and his players would not travel to Brisbane for the Fourth Test. To the disgust of the Australian team, the ABC eventually backed down and the game went ahead as planned. In a nail-biting match, tonsillitis sufferer Eddie Paynter left his hospital bed to hit an invaluable 83 in England's first innings. Jardine's team went on to win the Test, and with it the Ashes, by six wickets on the sixth and final day.

Back in Sydney, England confirmed their superiority with victory by eight wickets to seal a 4–1 series triumph. Highlights of the match included a battling 98 by nightwatchman Harold Larwood and a spell of 5–33 by left-arm spinner Hedley Verity as Australia collapsed in their second innings from 115–1 to 182 all out.

Although delighted by England's win, the MCC were eager to repair the damage caused by the 'Bodyline' controversy. Neither Larwood or Voce were picked for the next Ashes series in 1934, and the following year rules were introduced to make the leg-side fields Jardine had set against the Australians illegal. The 'Bodyline' episode was over, but the bitterness it caused would linger for many years.

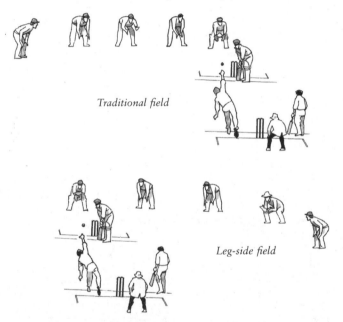

Traditional field

Leg-side field

First Test: Sydney, Dec 2–7
Australia 360 & 164, England 524 & 1–0
England won by 10 wickets

Second Test: Melbourne, Dec 30–Jan 3
Australia 228 & 191, England 169 & 139
Australia won by 111 runs

Third Test: Adelaide, Jan 13–18
England 341 & 412, Australia 222 & 193
England won by 338 runs

Fourth Test: Brisbane, Feb 10–16
Australia 340 & 175, England 356 & 162–4
England won by 6 wickets

Fifth Test: Sydney, Feb 23–28
Australia 435 & 182, England 454 & 168–2
England won by 8 wickets

Star performers

For Australia: Don Bradman, who averaged 56.57 with the bat, and Bill O'Reilly, who took 27 wickets at an average of 26.81.

For England: Paceman Harold Larwood, whose 33 wickets cost just 19.51 runs each, and batsmen Herbert Sutcliffe and Wally Hammond, both of whom averaged 55.

They said it

"What we saw in Australia in 1932/33 was something quite different, and really you could only say that the intention was to scare the daylights out of the batsman, and put him off his natural game."
Bill O'Reilly, who played for Australia during the 'Bodyline' series

"There are two sides out there. One is trying to play cricket, the other is not. The game is too good to be spoilt. It is time some people got out of it."
Australian captain **Bill Woodfull**, during the bitter Third Test

"Bodyline assuming such proportions as to menace the best interests of the game, making protection of the body by the batsman the main consideration. This is causing intensely bitter feeling between the players as well as injury. In our opinion it is unsportsmanlike. Unless stopped it is likely to upset the friendly relations between England and Australia."
Australian Board of Control telegram to England during the 'Bodyline' series

"We, Marylebone Cricket Club, deplore your cable."
MCC response to the ABC

"No one calls an Englishman unsportsmanlike and gets away with it."
England bowler **Gubby Allen**, who refused to bowl 'Bodyline'

"If someone had produced a batting helmet during the 'Bodyline' series, I would certainly have worn it."
Don Bradman

— ASHES 2005: THE STATS —

The 2005 Ashes series will mainly be remembered for the high quality of cricket it produced, some tense, edge-of-the-seat finishes and the wild celebrations that followed England's triumph. For a handful of anorak-clad fans, however, it was all about the stats. Here's a sample, just for them:

	England	Australia
Runs	2,962	2,810
Highest innings score	477	387
Run rate/over	3.9	3.7
Runs/per wicket	31.8	31.6
Wickets lost	93	89
Centuries	5	3
50s	14	9
Ducks	13	8
Balls per wicket taken	51	49
Catches	46	56
Run outs	4	0
No balls bowled	120	102

— CLANGERS —

Bat or field? It's the question numerous Ashes captains have pondered after winning the toss. On reflection, these skippers might feel they made the wrong choice:

- **Len Hutton, Brisbane 1954**
  England skipper Hutton won the toss and elected to field despite having lost wicketkeeper Godfrey Evans, who pulled out of the Test on the morning of the match through illness. His replacement, Test debutant Keith Andrew, endured a nightmare as England put down numerous catches in Australia's massive total of 601–8 declared.
  "We dropped a considerable number of catches, certainly double figures were reached if we count half-chances," recalled Andrew later. "Neither were we the fittest team in the world. [Denis] Compton broke a finger fielding on the first day and Alec Bedser was never well, as was proved when it was discovered that he had

developed shingles. One or two of us also got a touch of the sun, but there was no way of getting away from the fact that 'catches win matches'." Let down by their fielding, England lost by an innings.

- **Mike Denness, Edgbaston 1975**
  Denness was pilloried by the media after asking the Aussies to bat first in the opening Test of the 1975 series. The visitors scored 359 before twice dismissing England cheaply on a rain-affected pitch. The selectors were unimpressed and promptly sacked Denness, replacing him as captain with all-rounder Tony Greig.

- **David Gower, Headingley 1989**
  Aussie batsman Mark Taylor and Steve Waugh, who both scored centuries, left England captain Gower ruing his decision to put the tourists in. Buoyed by their flying start, Australia scored 601–7 declared and went on to win the match by 210 runs.

- **Nasser Hussain, Brisbane 2002**
  "I was so pessimistic about our chances of bowling the Aussies out twice I wanted to give our bowlers any little assistance that could possibly be found in the pitch," Hussain wrote in his autobiography, explaining his decision to field first. "And the only time when there might be anything in this pitch was on the first day." What was 'in' the pitch, though, was runs – 364 of them, to be precise, by the close of play on the first day. And, to make matters worse, England had taken just two wickets. After this flying start, Australia went on to win the match by 384 runs.

- **Ricky Ponting, Edgbaston 2005**
  Despite losing his main strike bowler, Glenn McGrath, to a freak injury doing practice, Australian skipper Ricky Ponting still decided to field first in the Second Test of the 2005 series. England responded by rattling up 407 by the close of play, a score which provided the platform for their eventual two-run victory.

- **Freddie Flintoff, Melbourne 2007**
  England skipper Flintoff saw his side dismissed for just 159 after electing to bat on a damp and unpredictable pitch. In reply, Australia scored 419 in better batting conditions and won by an innings.

— ASHES VICTORY: WHAT ARE THE ODDS ON THAT? —

Optimistic England fans who backed Michael Vaughan and co. to regain the Ashes in 2005 would have been quids in at the end of the series. At the start of the summer the bookies didn't much fancy

England's chances against the all-conquering Australians and offered odds of 5/1 for the home win. After the Aussies' emphatic win in the First Test at Lord's, England drifted out even further to 12/1, but the bookies were soon slashing their prices as the Three Lions fought back to triumph in the Second Test at Edgbaston. England's odds continued to fluctuate, mirroring the rollercoaster nature of this most unpredictable of Ashes series:

Date	Odds on England series win*
21 July (On morning of First Test at Lord's)	5/1
24 July (After Australia's victory in First Test)	12/1
7 August (After England's victory at Edgbaston)	3/1
15 August (After draw at Old Trafford)	3/1
28 August (After victory in Fourth Test at Trent Bridge)	4/7

* Odds provided by Betfair

— ASHES LEGENDS: JACK HOBBS —

One of the finest batsmen of all time, no English player has scored more runs or hit more centuries against the Aussies than Jack Hobbs.

The Surrey batsman thwarted the Australian bowlers for over 20 years, beginning with a well-made 83 on his Test debut in Melbourne in January 1908. In the years before World War One, during which he served in the Royal Flying Corps as an air mechanic, Hobbs was an enterprising, attacking stroke-maker, executing his shots with a mixture of power and finesse. Equally assured on hard, dry pitches of the type he encountered on his five tours of Australia or on English 'stickies', he was regarded as the most accomplished batsman of his generation. A major highlight of this pre-war period was the 1911/12 Ashes tour, during which Hobbs scored three consecutive centuries and helped England to a convincing 4–1 series victory.

After the war, a noticeably different Hobbs emerged: less dashing but more poised, and playing the majority of his shots off the back foot. Despite this transformation, the runs and the centuries – often scored in tandem with his England opening partner Herbert Sutcliffe – continued to flow. Remarkably, over half of his 197 first-class centuries were scored after he had turned 40, and in 1929 at Melbourne he became the oldest man ever, aged 46, to score a century in a Test match.

'The Master', as he was known, finally retired in 1934, having scored more first-class runs, 61,237, than any cricketer. Hobbs began a new career as a cricket journalist, and in 1953 became only the third cricketer to be knighted for his services to the sport. However, perhaps a greater accolade followed in 2000, some 37 years after his death, when Sir Jack was named by a 100-member panel of experts as one of the five Wisden Cricketers of the Century.

Jack Hobbs factfile
Born: Cambridge, 16 December 1882   **Died:** 21 December 1963
County: Surrey
Ashes Tests: 41 (1908–30)
Batting: 3,636 runs (ave 54.26)
Bowling: 0 wickets (53 runs conceded)

Others on Hobbs

"Jack Hobbs could have scored thousands more runs, but he often was content to throw his wicket away when he had reached his hundred and give someone else a chance."
England team-mate **Wilfred Rhodes**

"He was the most brilliant exponent of all time, and quite the best batsman of my generation on all types of wickets."
Herbert Sutcliffe, Hobbs' opening partner for England

'The Master'

— YOU DON'T WANT TO DO THAT! —

The last ten players to be out hit wicket in Ashes Tests:

Player	Year	Venue	Bowler	Score
Shane Warne (Aus)	2005	Edgbaston	Andrew Flintoff	42
Ashley Giles (Eng)	2005	Lord's	Brett Lee	11
John Crawley (Eng)	1997	Old Trafford	Glenn McGrath	83
Mike Atherton (Eng)	1997	Lord's	Michael Kasprowicz	77
Kim Hughes (Aus)	1981	The Oval	Ian Botham	31
Ian Redpath (Aus)	1975	Sydney	Fred Titmus	33
Norm O'Neill (Aus)	1961	Old Trafford	Fred Trueman	11
Denis Compton (Eng)	1948	Trent Bridge	Keith Miller	184
Denis Compton (Eng)	1947	Sydney	Ray Lindwall	17
Len Hutton (Eng)	1946	Sydney	Keith Miller	37

— BARMY TUNES —

England's Barmy Army of fans have built up quite a songbook in recent years. Here's a selection of their best Ashes ditties, courtesy of *www.barmyarmy.com*

Ricky Ponting
Ponting is the captain
Of the Aussie cricket team
But once the match is over
He is a gay drag queen

Ponting's special friend
Is a man called Glenn Mcgrath
You'll see them holding hands
At the Sydney Mardi Gras
(To the tune of 'My Old Man's a Dustman')

Take the Urn Home
So hoist up the John B sail
See how the mainsail sails
Call for the captain ashore
Take the urn home

We'll take the urn home
We'll take the urn home
With Strauss our captain
We'll take the urn home
(To the tune of 'Sloop John B')

Red-faced Captain
Ricky the red-faced captain
Leads a side in trouble and strife
Both he and Ryan Harris
Couldn't score to save their life

Strauss and his Pommie team-mates
Cookie, Bell and Kevin P
Showed how the Aussies are now
The worst team in their history
(To the tune of 'Rudolph the Red-nosed Reindeer')

Ashes stay at Lord's
Three Lions on our shirts
The Ashes urn still gleaming
Locked away at Lord's
And Ricky Ponting screaming
They stay at Lord's, they stay at Lord's, Ashes stay at Lord's
(repeat)
(To the tune of 'Three Lions')

Convict colony
In the town where I was born, there lived a man who was a thief
And he told me of his life, stealing bread and shagging sheep
So they put him in the nick, and then a magistrate he went to see
He said 'Put him on a ship, to the convict colony'
You all live in a convict colony, a convict colony, a convict colony
(repeat)
(To the tune of 'Yellow Submarine')

Freddie Flintoff
Oh Freddie is a giant
He wears an England cap
And when he faces Warney
He'll say 'I fancy that'
He'll smash him through the leg side
He'll smash him through the off

And if they ever get him out
We'll send in Darren Gough
(To the tune of 'My Old Man's a Dustman')

Ian Bell
Ian Bell, Ian Bell, fifty on the way
Oh what fun it is to see
The Aussies lose today
Ian Bell, Ian Bell, give us one more ton
Oh what fun it is to see
Convicts on the run
(To the tune of 'Jingle Bells')

Shane Warne
Shane Warne is an Aussie
He wears a baggy cap
He's got a Nike earring
He looks an Aussie prat
He's got his little flipper
He's got his box of tricks
But when he bowls to Freddie
He gets knocked for a six
(To the tune of 'My Old Man's a Dustman')

Mark Waugh
Mark Waugh is an Aussie,
He wears an Aussie hat
And when he saw the bookie's cash,
He said 'I'm having that'.
He shared it out with Warney.
They went and had some beers
And when the ACB found out,
They hushed it up for years!
(Also to the tune of 'My Old Man's a Dustman')

— THE GREAT ASHES SERIES:
'THE INVINCIBLES', ENGLAND 1948 —

The 1948 Australian touring party is regarded by many as the finest assembled in Ashes history. Captained by the incomparable Don Bradman, the team lived up to its nickname, 'The Invincibles', by demonstrating strength in every department. The batting, featuring fast-scoring run-getters like Arthur Morris, Lindsay Hassett and, of course, Bradman himself, was awesome; and the bowling, which included a trio of lively quicks in Ray Lindwall, Keith Miller and Bill Johnston, was just as impressive.

The tone of the series was set in the First Test at Trent Bridge. Johnston took 5–36 to dismiss England cheaply, the tourists responding with centuries from Bradman and Hassett to put themselves in control. For a while, a battling ton by Denis Compton held up the Aussies but, once he tumbled onto his wicket while trying to avoid a Miller bouncer, the result was never in doubt.

If anything, the Lord's Test was even more one-sided: centuries by Morris and Syd Barnes and eight wickets for Lindwall being highlights of a crushing win for the Aussies by 409 runs.

Another century by Compton raised England's hopes at Old Trafford but rain intervened after the tourists had put in an under-par batting display in their first innings and the match finished in a draw.

England's improved form continued in the Fourth Test at Headingley when, thanks to centuries by Cyril Washbrook and Bill Edrich, the home side posted 496 after batting first. Australia responded with 458, Neil Harvey hitting 112, and when England declared on the final morning another draw seemed likely. However, in an extraordinary run chase, which saw century-makers Morris and Bradman score at roughly four an over, the Aussies reached their unlikely target of 404 for the loss of just three wickets.

Even after that remarkable victory, there was no letup from Bradmen's men. In the final Test at The Oval, England were scuttled out for just 52, Lindwall taking 6–20, and did only marginally better in their second innings. In reply, Bradman was out for a second-ball duck in his last Test innings, but another big hundred from the in-form Morris ensured that 'The Invincibles' would end their unbeaten tour with another emphatic win.

First Test: Trent Bridge, June 10–15
England 165 & 441, Australia 509 & 98–2
Australia won by 8 wickets

Second Test: Lord's, June 24–29
Australia 350 & 460–7 dec, England 215 & 186
Australia won by 409 runs

Third Test: Old Tafford, July 8–13
England 363 & 174–3 dec, Australia 221 & 92–1
Match drawn

Fourth Test: Headingley, July 22–27
England 496 & 365–8 dec, Australia 458 & 404–3 dec
Australia won by 7 wickets

Fifth Test: The Oval, Aug 14–18
England 52 & 188, Australia 389
Australia won by an innings and 149 runs

Star performers

For England: The elegant Denis Compton provided home fans with much entertainment, averaging 62.44.

For Australia: Opening batsman Arthur Morris scored 696 runs at an average of 87, while fast bowlers Bill Johnston and Ray Lindwall both took 27 wickets.

They said it

"All England feels that now, at last, we may be able to fight for the Ashes on more equal terms again."
Bill Edrich, on Don Bradman's retirement

"Tell me, Mr Ferguson, do you use an adding machine when The Don comes out to bat?"
King George VI to the Australian scorer during the 1948 series

— WARNE'S BALL OF THE CENTURY —

Shane Warne's first ball in Ashes cricket, a big-spinning legbreak which pitched six inches outside of Mike Gatting's leg stump before viciously turning to clip the top of the England batsman's off stump, is probably the most famous delivery in the long history of England-Australia clashes.

With that dismissal, in the First Test at Old Trafford in 1993, Warne seemed to cast a spell over the English batsmen which they struggled to break thereafter. Certainly, Warne himself views his 'Ball of the Century' as a metaphorical as well as a literal turning point. "In the space of one delivery so much had changed," he said later. "My confidence was sky-high. I was pumped up and rock'n'rolling."

Naturally, Gatting has less fond memories of the ball that shook the cricketing world. Not only was he dismissed for just four runs, but much was made also of his portly physique in the days that followed. "How anyone can spin the ball the width of Gatting boggles the mind," suggested Martin Johnson in *The Independent*, while England captain Graham Gooch also joined in the fun, joking, "If it had been a cheese roll, it would never have got past him."

"If it had been a cheese roll it would never have got past him"

— SUBS DO FOR PONTING —

Somerset's James Hildreth and Durham's Gary Pratt were the two unsung heroes of England's 2005 Ashes victory, both sending Australian captain Ricky Ponting back to the pavilion while on the pitch as substitute fielders. Hildreth was the first to strike, catching Ponting for 42 in the second innings of the First Test at Lord's. However, Australia still went on to win the match comfortably.

If Hildreth's catch made little difference to the final result, the same could not be said of Pratt's run-out of Ponting at Trent Bridge in the Fourth Test. The dismissal, in the Australians' second innings, proved to be a pivotal moment in England's eventual three-wicket victory.

"I just wanted the ball to come to me every single ball," Pratt, who was fielding in place of the injured Simon Jones, recalled later. "I remember Damien Martyn dropping one down, shouting 'yes' and thinking to myself, 'right, that's me'. The ball was running along the square so I was able to pick it up cleanly. I had about one-and-a-half stumps in view and I just let go. I didn't ever think about missing. I knew from the moment it left my hand it was the one. It was quite a big moment in the series. I've seen the run-out a few times on video and it looks quite nice to be honest."

After his dismissal of Ponting, Pratt became something of a cult hero for England fans and his (small) part in the home side's triumph was officially recognised when he was included in the team's victory bus parade to Trafalgar Square. Among the huge crowds in the square was a group of supporters wearing 'Pratt for OBE' T-shirts, an indication of the fielder's new-found iconic status.

Ricky Ponting, on the other hand, was less enamoured of the Durham player, suggesting that England captain Michael Vaughan had bent the rules by using Pratt as a specialist fielder rather than as a legitimate substitute. This despite the fact that, in the previous Test at Old Trafford, Australian substitute fielder Brad Hodge had caught both Michael Vaughan and Kevin Pietersen! Much to the amusement of England fans, Ponting's sour diatribe had no effect other than to lumber the Aussie skipper with a fine of 75% of his £5,200 match fee. (See *Subs in the Limelight*, page 124)

— KEV'S SEVEN SIXES —

During his Ashes-winning innings of 158 at The Oval on 12 September 2005, Kevin Pietersen hit a record seven sixes, one more than England legend Ian Botham managed in his famous century at Old Trafford in 1981. Here's how Kev got after the Aussie bowlers – and got the fans in the stands ducking for cover . . .

Time	Bowler	Six hit
11.56am	Shane Warne	Lifted into the stands at deep mid-wicket to bring up the 100 for England.
11.59am	Shane Warne	Into the crowd at mid-wicket again off the final ball of the same Warne over.
13.22pm	Brett Lee	Pietersen hooks a short ball over the rope at deep fine leg.
13.30pm	Brett Lee	Another hook over square leg to bring up the 150 and Kev goes on to smash 16 off the over.
16.04pm	Brett Lee	A pull into the crowd over mid-wicket.
16.06pm	Shane Warne	Pietersen smashes the spinner for a huge straight six.
16.42pm	Shane Warne	A six over wide mid-on is followed by a four to take KP to a magnificent 150.

In total, Pietersen deposited 12 sixes into the crowd during the 2005 Ashes series – one more than England's other big-hitter, Andrew Flintoff.

— PROLIFIC PARTNERSHIPS —

Incredibly, Australian batsmen hold the record for the highest partnerships in Ashes cricket for all wickets except the last. Predictably, the name of Don Bradman figures prominently in the following list, the Aussie legend being involved in record stands for the second, third, fourth, fifth and sixth wickets. Of these, the one of 451 between Bradman (244) and his sidekick Bill Ponsford (266) for the second wicket at The Oval in 1934 is the highest in Ashes history.

The Australians really do seem to save their best for England – no fewer than six of their stands listed below are Aussie record partnerships against any country:

Wicket	Players	Venue	Year	Runs
1st	Geoff Marsh (138)			
	& Mark Taylor (219)	Trent Bridge	1989	329
2nd	Bill Ponsford (266)			
	& Don Bradman (244)	The Oval	1934	451
3rd	Don Bradman (187)			
	& Lindsay Hassett (128)	Brisbane	1946	276
4th	Bill Ponsford (181)			
	& Don Bradman (304)	Headingley	1934	388
5th	Sid Barnes (234)			
	& Don Bradman (234)	Sydney	1946	405
6th	Jack Fingleton (136)			
	& Don Bradman (270)	Melbourne	1937	346
7th	Clem Hill (188)			
	& Hugh Trumble (46)	Melbourne	1898	165
8th	Roger Hartigan (116)			
	& Clem Hill (160)	Adelaide	1908	243
9th	Syd Gregory (201)			
	& Jack Blackham (74)	Sydney	1894	154
10th	Tip Foster (287)			
	& Wilfred Rhodes (40*)			
	(Eng)	Sydney	1903	130

* not out

— ASHES LEGENDS: STAN MCCABE —

A stockily-built attacking batsman and useful change bowler, Stan McCabe was an ever present in Ashes Tests from 1930 until the outbreak of World War II.

Although he scored many of his runs with drives in front of the wicket, McCabe was also an excellent hooker. His ability to score off short-pitched bowling proved especially useful in the Bodyline series of 1932/33, when the English bowlers fired a barrage of bouncers at the Australian batsmen. While his team-mates struggled to cope with this new tactic in the First Test at Sydney, McCabe responded by going on the counter-attack. Resuming his innings, he courageously told his father, "If I happen to get hit out there Dad, keep Mum from jumping the fence and laying into those Pommie bowlers." When the last Australian batsman was out McCabe was still there on 187 not out, and was hailed as a hero by the home crowd.

McCabe's other great innings against England came six years later at Trent Bridge, a brilliant knock of 232 scored at a run a minute. His captain, Don Bradman, was so impressed by McCabe's magnificent display of forceful batting that he told the rest of the Australian side, "Come and see this. Don't miss a minute of it. You'll never see the likes of this again." When McCabe was eventually out Bradman personally congratulated him on the pavilion steps, saying, "If I could play an innings like that, I'd be a proud man, Stan."

McCabe's Test career was ended by World War II when he was still at his peak. He died at the age of 58 after falling off a cliff while dispensing with a dead possum near his home in Sydney, but his huge contribution to Aussie cricket was posthumously recognised in 2002 when he was inducted into the Australian Cricket Hall of Fame.

Stan McCabe factfile
Born: Grenfell, New South Wales, 16 July 1910
Died: 25 August 1968
State: New South Wales
Ashes Tests: 24 (1930–38)
Batting: 2,031 runs (ave 50.78)
Bowling: 21 wickets (ave 51.24)

Others on McCabe

"It would be hard to think of a greater Australian batsman. He had qualities that even Bradman hadn't got."
Sir Len Hutton

"One of his great points was that he never bothered about averages; he enjoyed his batting. He was one of the two or three great batsmen I saw."
Sir Robert Menzies, former Australian Prime Minister

— FOSTER'S FLYING START —

No batsman has had a better Ashes debut than England's Reginald 'Tip' Foster, who hit 287 at Sydney in 1903. The colossal score remains the highest by a batsman on his debut and the highest by an Englishman in Australia. In the same innings Foster also put on 130 for the last wicket with Wilfred Rhodes to set another Ashes record. Thanks largely to Foster's superb debut innings, England went on to win the match by five wickets.

Foster, who also played in five football internationals for England, went on to appear in eight Tests before his premature death from diabetes at the age of 36.

— HOWZAT! —

Legendary Australian wicketkeeper Rodney Marsh holds the record for the number of dismissals by a fielder in Ashes matches, with a total of 148 (141 caught and seven stumped). Marsh made his Ashes debut in the First Test in Brisbane in 1970 and, in the same match, claimed his first victim when he caught England opener Geoff Boycott for 37 off the bowling of John Gleeson. Thirteen years later the extravagantly mustachioed wicketkeeper dismissed his last Englishman, catching Eddie Hemmings in the Fifth Test in Sydney in January 1983.

Wicketkeeper	Ashes Tests	Caught	Stumped	Total
Rodney Marsh (Aus)	42	141	7	148
Ian Healy (Aus)	33	123	12	135
Alan Knott (Eng)	34	97	8	105
Adam Gilchrist (Aus)	20	89	7	96
Bert Oldfield (Aus)	38	59	31	90
Dick Lilley (Eng)	32	65	19	84
Alec Stewart (Eng)	33	82	2	84

— ENGLAND: BEST ASHES NICKNAME XI —

1. Jack 'The Master' Hobbs (1908–30)
2. WG 'The Doctor' Grace (1880–99)
3. Colin 'The Kipper' Cowdrey (1954–75)
4. John 'Creepy' Crawley (1995–2003)
5. Keith 'The Gnome' Fletcher (1968–75)
6. Ian 'Beefy' Botham (1977–89)
7. Frank 'Typhoon' Tyson (1954–59)
8. Ashley 'King of Spain' Giles (2001–06)
9. Darren 'Rhino' Gough (1994–2001)
10. Matthew 'Shrek' Hoggard (2002–07)
11. Phil 'The Cat' Tufnell (1990–2001)

Ashley Giles' unusual nickname stems from 2004 when his county, Warwickshire, ordered a set of mugs bearing the slogan 'King of Spin' for the player's testimonial season. However, the manufacturers were clearly not cricket fans as the mugs they produced were labelled, 'Ashley Giles, King of Spain'. Giles' team-mates latched onto his new tag and the nickname soon transferred to the England fans, some of whom carried Spanish flags in support of the spinner during the 2005 Ashes series.

— BROTHERS IN ARMS —

A number of brothers have played together in Ashes matches and they are:

Australia
Dave and Ned Gregory (1 Test, 1877)
Charles and Alec Bannerman (1 Test, 1879)
Ian and Greg Chappell (22 Tests, 1970–80)*
Steve and Mark Waugh (26 Tests, 1993–2001)
* Another brother, Trevor, played three Tests against England in 1981

England
WG, EM and Fred Grace (1 Test, 1880)
Adam and Ben Hollioake (1 Test, 1997)

— CLIFFHANGERS —

The narrowest Ashes Test victories by runs:

Year	Venue	Result
2005	Edgbaston	England (407 & 182) beat Australia (308 & 279) by 2 runs
1902	Old Trafford	Australia (299 & 86) beat England (262 & 120) by 3 runs
1982	Melbourne	England (284 & 294) beat Australia (287 & 288) by 3 runs
1885	Sydney	Australia (181 & 165) beat England (133 & 207) by 6 runs
1882	The Oval	Australia (63 & 122) beat England (101 & 77) by 7 runs
1894	Sydney	England (325 & 437) beat Australia (586 & 186) by 10 runs

The narrowest Ashes Test victories by wickets:

Year	Venue	Result
1902	The Oval	England beat Australia by one wicket
1908	Melbourne	England beat Australia by one wicket

In the first of these victories, England required 15 runs when last man Wilfred Rhodes joined George Hirst in the middle. According to cricketing legend, the two Yorkshiremen told each other that "we can get 'em in singles", but Hirst always denied that the pair uttered the famous words. Whatever the plan, it certainly worked.

If anything, England's triumph in the Second Test in Melbourne six years later was even more remarkable. The visitors looked destined to lose, but England's last wicket pair Sydney Barnes and Arthur Fielder put on 39 runs together to secure an unlikely victory.

— A DECLARATION TOO SOON —

If only England skipper Andrew Flintoff had batted on, rather than declaring, in his side's first innings in the Second Test at Adelaide the Three Lions might have avoided defeat in at least one of the matches during the 2006/07 Ashes series.

As it turned out, England's total of 551–6 dec stands as the largest in Test cricket by a losing side batting first and declaring. Helped by a second innings England batting collapse, Australia went on to win the match by six wickets.

— ASHES TO ASHES —

Ashes cricketers who committed suicide include:

William Scotton (Eng): shot himself, aged 37, 9 July 1893
Arthur Shrewsbury (Eng): shot himself, aged 47, 19 May 1903
Albert Trott (Aus): shot himself, aged 41, 30 July 1914
Andrew Stoddart (Eng): shot himself, aged 52, 4 April 1915
Billy Bruce (Aus): drowned himself, aged 61, 3 August 1925
Albert Relf (Eng): shot himself, aged 62, 26 March 1937
John Iverson (Aus): shot himself, aged 58, 24 October 1973
Sid Barnes (Aus): poisoned himself, aged 61, 16 December 1973
Jim Burke (Aus): shot himself, aged 48, 2 February 1979
David Bairstow (Eng): hanged himself, aged 46, 5 January 1998

— SCRAPING THE BARREL FOR WOOD —

England's decision to tour Australia in 1887 with just 11 players backfired when medium-fast bowler Billy Barnes injured an arm after the First Test. The injury came about in bizarre circumstances when Barnes, who had taken 6–28 in Australia's second innings to enable England to win the match in Sydney by just 13 runs, got involved in a post-match argument with Aussie captain Percy McDonnell. During a robust exchange of opinions, Barnes aimed a punch at his opponent but only succeeded in banging his fist against a brick wall. The wall was undamaged; unfortunately for England, Barnes' hand wasn't. (See *Unlikely Injuries,* page 119)

A man short for the Second and final Test, also in Sydney, the tourists desperately searched around for a replacement for the fiery Barnes. Eventually, England managed to recruit one Reg Wood, a former Lancashire cricketer of no great reputation, who had emigrated to Australia and, at the time, was working at Melbourne Cricket Ground. Unsurprisingly, perhaps, Wood's contribution to the England cause proved to be minimal: he didn't bowl, didn't take a catch in the field and, batting at number ten, scored just six runs in his two completed innings. Nonetheless, England still won the Test by 71 runs to clinch victory in the series. As for Wood, he quickly returned to obscurity, never playing in another first-class match.

— BOYCS' BATTING MARATHON —

In the 1977 Trent Bridge Test, England's limpet-like opener Geoff Boycott set a new Ashes record by batting on all five days of the match. After the Australians had been dismissed for 243, the gritty Yorkshire batsman ended the first day on one not out. Amazingly, Boycott batted all through the next day, taking his score to 88 not out at stumps. Boycott was finally out for 107 on the third day of the Test, but had his pads back on the following day, reaching 38 not out by close of play. On the final day, Boycott continued to frustrate the Australian bowlers, finishing on 80 not out as England won the match by seven wickets.

Three years later, in the Centenary Test at Lord's in 1980, Australia's Kim Hughes matched Boycott's feat by batting on all five days. However, the fact that much of the match was lost to rain made this more of a statistical quirk than a genuine achievement.

— THE FIRST CENTURIONS —

Charles Bannerman scored the first century for Australia, hitting 165 in the inaugural Test match against England at Melbourne in March 1877. The Aussie opener might well have gone on to score the first double hundred, but he was forced to retire hurt after a delivery from England bowler George Ulyett broke one of his fingers.

Bannerman's score, out of an Australian total of 245, meant that he notched an incredible 67.35% of his side's runs. No other batsman in the history of Test cricket has ever dominated an innings to the same extent, and the home crowd was certainly appreciative of his efforts, raising £83, seven shillings and sixpence for the new hero. A forceful stroke-playing batsman, Bannerman should have gone on to become one of the early greats of Test cricket, but he retired after just three matches. The official reason for his departure from the international scene was ill health, but there were also suggestions that Bannerman was uncomfortable with his new-found celebrity status and had problems with drink and gambling. Happily, he later returned to Test cricket as an umpire, officiating in a number of England-Australia clashes.

England's first century was scored by the legendary WG Grace in the one-off Oval Test of 1880. Opening the batting with his brother Edward, the 32-year-old Grace hit 152 in England's first innings total of 420 and, together with Alfred 'Bunny' Lucas, put on 120 for the second wicket to record Test cricket's first century stand. Grace's ton provided the platform for England to win the Test by five wickets.

— 100 BEFORE LUNCH —

The cucumber sandwiches would have tasted especially delicious for these three Australian batsman, all of whom scored hundreds before lunch on the opening day of an Ashes Test:

Player	Year score	Venue score	Lunch	Final
Victor Trumper	1902	Old Trafford	103*	104
Charles Macartney	1926	Headingley	112*	151
Don Bradman	1930	Headingley	105*	334

* not out

— RUN FEAST AND FAMINE —

Spectators at the 1921 timeless Test (no time limit was set for completion of the match) in Adelaide had value for money as they saw England and Australia score a total of 1,753 runs – a record for an Ashes match. No fewer than six batsmen helped themselves to centuries, Australia's Herbie Collins top scoring with 162 in his side's first innings. Australia eventually won the match by 119 runs on the sixth day of play.

By contrast, runs were in short supply at Lord's in 1888 after heavy rain delayed the start and turned the wicket into a near-unplayable 'sticky'. Australia struggled to 116 all out in their first innings before dismissing England for a mere 53 runs. The Aussies fared little better in their second innings, amassing just 60 runs, to set England a victory target of 124. Opening for the home side, WG Grace hit the highest individual score of the match, 24, but the other batsmen failed to support him and England were all out for a miserable total of 62. The 291 runs scored in the four innings remains an all-time low for an Ashes Test.

— ASHES LEGENDS: HAROLD LARWOOD —

A fast and accurate pace bowler with a classical action, Harold Larwood was a key figure in the infamous Bodyline series of 1932/33.

Instructed by his captain, Douglas Jardine, to bowl 'leg theory' – short-pitched deliveries aimed at the batsman's body, supported by a strong leg-side field – Larwood and his Nottinghamshire team-mate Bill Voce responded enthusiastically, unleashing a barrage of bouncers at the Aussies. Larwood's bouncer was especially difficult to play, his lack of inches – he was only 5ft 9ins – resulting in a delivery which tended to skid into the batsman's ribs rather than rise safely over his head. Inevitably, not all his opponents were able to avoid these 90 mph missiles, and in the Third Test at Adelaide in 1933 two Australian batsmen, captain Bill Woodfull and wicketkeeper Bert Oldfield, were struck by Larwood. These incidents prompted the Australian Cricket Board to protest about England's aggressive tactics in a famously angry telegram to the MCC and, for a while, there was some doubt that the tour would continue. Happily for Larwood it did, as his 33 wickets helped England to an emphatic 4–1 series victory.

Larwood returned to England as a popular hero, but he received a more frosty reception from the MCC bigwigs, who were eager to repair the damaged relationship with their Australian counterparts. As the man most associated with Bodyline, Larwood was asked to sign a letter of apology to the Australian Cricket Board. He refused, insisting that he had simply been following the instructions of his captain. After being left out of the First Test against Australia in 1934, allegedly because of a foot injury, Larwood announced his retirement from international cricket. "I refuse to play any more Tests," he said. "I am unrepentant about leg theory. There is a big hush-hush campaign to bury leg theory and brand me as a dangerous and unfair bowler." The Test career of Larwood, a former miner, was over at the age of 28.

Ironically, shortly after World War II, he emigrated with his family to Australia, living happily in the country which once reviled him until his death in 1995.

Harold Larwood factfile
Born: Nuncargate, Notts, 14 November 1904   **Died:** 22 July 1995
County: Notts
Ashes Tests: 15 (1926–33)
Batting: 386 runs (ave 19.30)
Bowling: 64 wickets (ave 29.87)

Others on Larwood
"The chief trouble for the Australians today is that Larwood is a really
first-class fast bowler, and that he has developed leg theory better than
anyone else in the past."
Douglas Jardine in his book *Quest For The Ashes*, 1933

"He's too fast for me."
Australian batsman **Alan Kippax**, during the Bodyline series

*Larwood goes
for the jugular*

— CAUGHT IN THE SLIPS —

Former Australia captain Greg Chappell holds the record for the most
catches by a fielder in Ashes matches with 61, four ahead of fellow
Aussie Allan Border and England's Ian Botham. Chappell's first victim
was Colin Cowdrey, whom he caught off his own bowling in his debut

Test at Perth in 1970. Thirteen years later in Sydney he made his last Ashes catch, claiming the prize wicket of David Gower from a delivery by Geoff Lawson. Chappell also holds the record for the most catches in an Ashes Test by a non-wicketkeeper, taking seven at Perth in 1974.

— PONTING'S HORRORSHOW —

The 2010/11 Ashes series was one to forget for the Australians, but for skipper Ricky Ponting it proved to be a nightmare almost without end. Generally regarded as his country's best batsman, Ponting had a torrid time at the crease from start to finish and ended the series with a paltry average of 16.14 – the lowest by an Aussie captain in the Ashes since Brian Booth in 1965/66. "My series has been horrible, there's no two ways about it," he admitted afterwards.

Even worse, his side's 3–1 series loss meant that Ponting became only the second Australian captain (after Billy Murdoch in the 1880s) to preside over three Ashes defeats, following previous humblings by the Old Enemy in 2005 and 2009.

Little wonder, then, that in March 2011 Ponting bowed to the inevitable and resigned as his country's skipper after seven years in charge of the Baggy Greens.

— RUNNING RIOT —

England comfortably hold the record for the highest score in an Ashes innings, notching 903–7 declared in the Fourth Test at The Oval in 1938. The score remained a world record for a single innings in Test cricket until 1997 when Sri Lanka scored 952–6 declared against India at Colombo.

The Oval match is most often remembered for Len Hutton's then record score of 364 but Maurice Leyland (187), Wally Hammond (59), Joe Hardstaff junior (169 not out) and Arthur Wood (53) also made valuable contributions to the home side's mammoth total.

Skipper Hammond had gambled on winning the toss and batting, selecting a team with just three recognised bowlers. With such a strong batting line up, England might well have hit four figures had Hammond not declared – prompting a furious reaction from Oval groundsman 'Bosser' Martin, who believed that a score of 1,000 plus would be a fitting tribute to his perfect batting pitches. In fact, the England skipper probably would have batted on but for injuries to Aussie batsman Jack Fingleton and Don Bradman. With neither player able to bat, Hammond calculated that 900 or so runs would be sufficient for England to enforce the follow on. And so it proved: a demoralised Australia were dismissed for 201 and 123, enabling England to record a comprehensive win by an innings and 579 runs.

Including, The Oval run-athon, the top ten team scores in Ashes history are:

Year	Team	Venue	Total	Highest Score
1938	England	The Oval	903–7 dec	Len Hutton, 364
1930	Australia	Lord's	729–6 dec	Don Bradman, 254
1934	Australia	The Oval	701	Bill Ponsford, 266
1930	Australia	The Oval	695	Don Bradman, 232
2009	Australia	Cardiff	674–6 dec	Ricky Ponting, 150
1946	Australia	Sydney	659–8 dec	Sid Barnes, Don Bradman, 234
1938	England	Trent Bridge	658–8 dec	Eddie Paynter, 216*
1964	Australia	Old Trafford	656–8 dec	Bobby Simpson, 311
1993	Australia	Headingley	653–4 dec	Allan Border, 200*
1948	Australia	Brisbane	645	Don Bradman, 187

* not out

— MOST WICKETS IN AN ASHES SERIES —

Spin king Jim Laker holds the record for the number of wickets in an Ashes series with 46 in 1956. The England bowler's impressive haul famously included 19 wickets in the Fourth Test at Old Trafford to set a world record which remains unbeaten today. (See *Jim Has Aussies In A Spin*, page 78)

Terry Alderman tops the Australian wicket-taking charts with 42 in the 1981 series in England, a figure the paceman came close to matching eight years later:

Player	Wickets	Tests	Balls	Runs	BB	Ave
Jim Laker (Eng, 1956)	46	5	1,703	442	10–53	9.60
Terry Alderman (Aus, 1981)	42	6	1,950	893	6–135	21.26
Rodney Hogg (Aus, 1978/79)	41	6	1,740	527	6–74	12.85
Terry Alderman (Aus, 1989)	41	6	1,616	712	6–128	17.36
Shane Warne (Aus, 2005)	40	5	1,517	797	6–46	19.92

— THEY SAID IT 1 —

A selection of Ashes-related quotes from the northern and southern hemispheres:

"The other advantage England have got when Phil Tufnell's bowling is that he isn't fielding."
Former Australia captain **Ian Chappell** has a dig at the England spinner during the 1990/91 Ashes series

"Geoffrey is the only fellow I've met who fell in love with himself at a young age and has remained faithful ever since."
Former Aussie paceman **Dennis Lillee** on Geoffrey Boycott

"If I were being polite, I'd say that Gatt is a little long in the tooth, somewhat immobile and carries too much weight. But I prefer straight talking, so I'm saying what I really think. Gatt is too old, too slow and too fat."
Geoff Boycott on Mike Gatting's recall to the England team for the 1993 Ashes series

"A fart competing with thunder."
England captain **Graham Gooch** on England's chances against Australia in the 1990/91 series 'Down Under'

"We were a bit like Bolton [Wanderers]. We had to make our whole greater than its individual parts."
Nasser Hussain on his time as England captain

"I'm not talking to anyone in the British media – they're all pricks."
Straight talking from Australian captain **Allan Border**, 1993

"Man for man, on paper, the Australian side stand out like dogs' balls."
Former Australian captain **Greg Chappell** before the 1994 Ashes series

"A six-foot blond-haired beach bum bowling at 90mph trying to knock your head off and then telling you you're a feeble-minded tosser."
Mike Atherton's view of Ashes cricket

"A cricket tour in Australia would be the most delightful period in your life – if you were deaf."
Harold Larwood

— THE GREAT ASHES SERIES: 'LAKER ON TOP', ENGLAND 1956 —

The 1956 series produced some of the most dramatic moments in Ashes history, and is remembered, above all, for arguably the single most extraordinary individual performance in Test match cricket.

Little of the drama that was to follow, however, was suggested by the First Test at Trent Bridge – a slow-scoring, rain-affected draw. The Second Test saw England's Lord's hoodoo strike again, as the home side were twice dismissed cheaply and lost by 185 runs. The key performers for Australia were spinner Richie Benaud, who hit a swashbuckling 97 in the second innings, and pace bowler Keith Miller, who took ten wickets in the match for the only time in his Test career.

For the Third Test at Headingley England surprisingly recalled Cyril Washbrook after a five-year absence (See *Recall of the Old Codgers*, page 133). Partnered by England captain and century-maker Peter May, the 41-year-old Washbrook put on 187 for England's fourth wicket in a total of 325. On a turning pitch, spinners Jim Laker and Tony Lock then took 18 wickets between them as Australia went down to an innings defeat.

Laker, though, was only warming up. At Old Trafford, he returned the incredible figures of 19–90, taking all of his wickets at the Stretford End. Following centuries by Peter Richardson and the recalled Reverend

David Sheppard, Laker's hypnotic bowling gave England another innings victory to clinch Peter May's side hold on the Ashes.

Laker was among the wickets again in the final Test at The Oval, taking another seven to lift his series total to an Ashes record 46. The match, however, finished in a draw after Australia struggled to 27–5 having been set 228 to win.

> **First Test: Trent Bridge, June 7–12**
> England 217–8 dec & 188–3 dec, Australia 148 & 120–3
> Match drawn
>
> **Second Test: Lord's, June 21–26**
> Australia 285 & 257, England 171 & 186
> **Australia** won by 185 runs
>
> **Third Test: Headingley, July 12–17**
> England 325, Australia 143 & 140
> **England** won by an innings and 42 runs
>
> **Fourth Test: Old Trafford, July 26–31**
> England 459, Australia 84 & 205
> **England** won by an innings and 170 runs
>
> **Fifth Test: The Oval, Aug 23–28**
> England 247 & 182–3 dec, Australia 202 & 27–5
> Match drawn

Star performers

For England: Jim Laker, whose 46 wicket haul remains a record for an Ashes series.

For Australia: Fast bowler Keith Miller collected 21 wickets while also contributing over 200 runs with the bat.

They said it

"It [Laker's] was an extraordinary performance and an unpalatable loss, one that Neil Harvey and I vowed to reverse the next time we toured England."
Australian leg spinner **Richie Benaud**

"No writer of boys' fiction would so strain romantic credulity as to make his hero, playing for England against Australia, capture nine first-innings wickets; then help himself to all ten in the second innings."
Cricket writer **Neville Cardus**

— CATCHES WIN MATCHES – OR DO THEY? —

A striking feature of the 2005 Ashes was the number of catches dropped by both teams, but especially by England. In the five Tests Michael Vaughan's side missed a total of 25 chances, with wicketkeeper Geraint Jones (7) and Kevin Pietersen (6) being the worst offenders. Fortunately for England, these fielding blunders proved less costly than they might have been, as the dropped Aussies only added another 502 additional runs after being given a second chance. (See *Kev's Butterfingers*, page 137)

England, on the other hand, took full advantage of the 17 Australian dropped catches, adding a total of 983 extra runs. Adam Gilchrist and Shane Warne committed the most costly errors for the Aussies, dropping Kevin Pietersen when he was on 0 and 15 respectively in the second innings of the final Test at The Oval. Pietersen went on to secure the Ashes for England by hitting a brilliant 158.

— ASHES 2010/11: A RECORD-BREAKING SERIES —

The 2010/11 Ashes series in Australia saw numerous records tumble and, happily for England, most of the new landmarks were set by the tourists. Here's a selection of some of the most significant ones:

- In the First Test at Brisbane Aussie batsmen Michael Hussey and Brad Haddin shared a partnership of 307, a record for the sixth wicket at The Gabba.
- In England's second innings of the same match, opener Alastair Cook scored 235 not out, breaking Don Bradman's record for the highest Test score at The Gabba.
- At the close of the second day of the Second Test at Adelaide, Cook was 136 not out. Combined with his innings at Brisbane, the opener had amassed an incredible 371 runs in 1,022 minutes to set a new record for England for runs scored and minutes at the crease without being dismissed.
- When the tourists followed their score of 517–1 declared at The Gabba with a total of 620–5 declared at Adelaide, it was the first time in Ashes history that England had scored more than 500 runs in consecutive innings.
- In the Fourth Test at Melbourne, Australia were dismissed for 98 in their first innings – their lowest ever total at the MCG and their lowest in a home Ashes Test since 1888.
- In the Fifth Test at Sydney England scored 644 – their highest total ever in an Ashes Test in Australia.

- In the same innings England's sixth, seventh and eighth wickets all put on a 100 runs or more, the first time this had happened in Test cricket.
- England's three Test victories in the series were all by an innings, the first time this feat had been achieved by a touring team in the history of Test cricket.
- During the series the tourists nine hundreds were made by six different batsmen, a record for England in the Ashes.
- For the first time in the Ashes England passed the 500-mark four times in the same series.

— ASHES LEGENDS: DENIS COMPTON —

One of a select band of players to make a hundred on his Ashes debut, Denis Compton was a dashing, stroke-playing batsman who charmed and delighted crowds with his entertaining approach to the game.

Compton was only 19 when he first played against the Australians in 1938, scoring 102 at Trent Bridge and, in the following Test, a match-saving 76 not out on a damp, difficult pitch at Lord's. The young Middlesex batsman's career was soon interrupted by World War II, much of which he spent serving in the army in India. After the war Compton went on his first tour of Australia, scoring centuries in both innings of the Adelaide Test in 1947. Later that year he enjoyed a golden summer, hitting 18 centuries as Middlesex won the County Championship. Resuming acquaintances with the Australians, Compton scored two big centuries in the 1948 series but was powerless to stop Bradman's side winning the series at a canter.

Fittingly, when England eventually reclaimed the Ashes in 1953 it was Compton who struck the winning boundary at The Oval. Despite a chronic knee problem he continued to play for England until 1957, his stylish and exuberant batsmanship remaining unaffected by the passage of the years.

Compton's knee injury was sustained in a collision with the Charlton goalkeeper while playing football for Arsenal, with whom he won the league championship in 1948 and the FA Cup in 1950. A talented winger, he also played for England in 12 wartime football internationals but was never capped in an official peacetime match. Hugely popular among both cricket and football fans, Compton was one of the first sportsmen to cash in on his appeal, famously becoming the public face of Brylcreem.

Following his retirement, Compton worked as a cricket commentator for the BBC and had a column in *The Sunday Express*. He died in 1997 but his name lives on, most notably in the form of the Compton-Miller Trophy which is awarded to the player of the series in England-Australia encounters.

Denis Compton factfile
Born: Hendon, 23 May 1918   **Died:** 23 April 1997
County: Middlesex
Ashes Tests: 28 (1938–56)
Batting: 1,842 runs (ave 43.86)
Bowling: 3 wickets (ave 79.33)

Others on Compton

"To watch Denis Compton play cricket on a good day was to know what joy was."
John Major, speaking at Compton's memorial service in 1997

"The only player to call his partner for a run and wish him good luck at the same time."
John Warr, Middlesex team-mate

*The majestic
Denis Compton*

— TOP WICKET TAKERS —

Aussie phenomenon Shane Warne is the leading wicket taker in Ashes history, with 195 scalps to his name. The leg spinner's first victim was veteran batsman Mike Gatting, who he famously bowled round his legs with 'the ball of the century' in the First Test at Old Trafford in 1993 – Warne's very first delivery in Ashes cricket. After that, Warne terrorised English batsmen on a regular basis, finally passing Dennis Lillee's longstanding Ashes wicket haul in The Oval Test in 2005 when he trapped Marcus Trescothick lbw in England's second innings.

England's leading wicket taker in Ashes Tests, meanwhile, is Ian Botham, who claimed 148 Aussie scalps between 1977 and 1989.

Bowler	Tests	Wickets	Ave	Best bowling
Shane Warne (Aus)	36	195	23.25	8–71
Dennis Lillee (Aus)	29	167	21.00	7–89
Glenn McGrath (Aus)	30	157	20.93	8–38
Ian Botham (Eng)	36	148	27.65	6–78
Hugh Trumble (Aus)	31	141	20.88	8–65
Bob Willis (Eng)	35	128	26.14	8–43
Monty Noble (Aus)	39	115	24.86	7–17
Ray Lindwall (Aus)	29	114	22.44	7–63
Wilfred Rhodes (Eng)	41	109	24.00	8–68

— THIRD UMPIRE FIRST —

The third umpire system was first used in the Ashes in England in 1993, with former Yorkshire and Leicestershire batsman Chris Balderstone taking on the role of the third official for the First Test at Lord's.

Communicating with on-field umpires David Shepherd and Mervyn Kitchen via radio, Balderstone's role was limited to making decisions on run-outs, stumpings and hit wicket after watching a TV replay of the incident. When he ruled that Robin Smith had been stumped off the bowling of Aussie spinner Tim May the South African-born batsman became the first player to be dismissed by a third umpire in a Test match in England.

— MEN OF THE MATCH 2009 —

Test	Venue	Man of the Match
First	Cardiff	Ricky Ponting (Aus)
Second	Lord's	Andrew Flintoff (Eng)
Third	Edgbaston	Michael Clarke (Aus)
Fourth	Headingley	Marcus North (Aus)
Fifth	The Oval	Stuart Broad (Eng)

In addition to these awards, England captain Andrew Strauss was named Man of the Series.

— GOOCHIE'S STRANGE DISMISSAL —

Players have been caught, bowled, run out, stumped, given out lbw and hit wicket in Ashes matches, but none had been dismissed for 'handling the ball' until Graham Gooch received his marching orders for that little-known contravention of cricket's laws on the last day of the First Test at Old Trafford in 1993.

The England opener had passed the century mark and the match appeared to be heading for a draw when Aussie bowler Merv Hughes got a delivery to lift sharply off the pitch. Gooch successfully fended the ball into the ground but then looked on in horror as it bounced menacingly towards his stumps. Instinctively, the England skipper flicked the ball away with the back of his hand, an action which led to loud appeals from those Aussies who were up on the more obscure laws of the game. Umpire Dickie Bird, a lifetime student of cricket's rulebook, instantly raised his finger and Gooch became only the fifth batsman in the history of Test cricket to be given out 'handled the ball'.

The unusual dismissal proved to be a turning point as England slumped from 223–3 to 332 all out, providing Australia with victory by 179 runs.

— TED'S RALLYING CALL —

After England lost the first two Tests of the 1989 Ashes series, Ted Dexter, the chairman of the England selectors, attempted to lift the team's spirits by penning the following ditty to the tune of 'Onward, Christian Soldiers':

> Onward Gower's cricketers
> Striving for a score,
> With our bats uplifted,
> We want more and more,
> Alderman the master,
> Represents the foe,
> Forward into battle,
> Down the pitch we go

Dexter suggested the team should sing the song in the bath at the top of their voices and – who knows? – the positive lyrics may have helped 'Gower's cricketers' claim a morale-boosting draw in the Third Test at Edgbaston. By the end of the series, however, England had been stuffed 4–0, Dexter was rambling about the 'planetary arrangements' not being in England's favour and Gower had resigned as team captain. Dexter may have demanded 'more and more' but, despite calling up 29 different players during the series, he'd got 'less and less'.

— DOUBLE ENTENDRE ASHES XI —

Taking our cue from commentator Brian Johnston's immortal line, 'The bowler's Holding, the batsman's Willey' we present an Ashes eleven whose surnames score highly on the snigger-ometer:

1. Leslie Gay (Eng, 1894)
2. Jack Badcock (Aus, 1936–38)
3. Arthur Fagg (Eng, 1936)
4. Jack Crapp (Eng, 1948)
5. David Sincock (Aus, 1966)
6. Peter Willey (Eng, 1980–85)
7. Graeme Hole (Aus, 1951–55))
8. Charles Studd (Eng, 1882–83)
9. Alec Coxon (Eng, 1948)
10. Joe Hardstaff snr (Eng, 1907–08)
11. Pat Pocock (Eng, 1968)

— LEN'S RUN RECORD —

Legendary England opener Sir Len Hutton holds the record for the highest individual score in an Ashes contest. His 364 at The Oval in 1938, compiled over 13 hours and 20 minutes of intense concentration during England's record innings total of 903–7 declared, beat Don Bradman's previous Ashes record of 334 at Headingley in 1930 and has not been seriously challenged since in an England-Australia match. Hutton's runs came from 35 fours, 15 threes, 18 twos and 143 singles, and the total stood as a world Test best for 20 years, until West Indian all-rounder Gary Sobers scored 365 not out against Pakistan in 1958.

Speaking about his record-breaking innings in 1978, Hutton recalled: "I don't think the idea of trying for Don's record came into my head until I was around 250. By the Monday night, however, the strain was beginning to tell. In fact, Maurice Leyland told me I would probably have difficulty in sleeping and he advised me to drink a port and Guinness. I was then a strict teetotaller but I did as he suggested. It was no good. I should have had five or six. With so many people telling me that I needed another 35 runs to break the record, I tossed and turned most of the night."

The next morning, Hutton inched towards the record, his every run being cheered to the rafters. "In the end Fleetwood-Smith bowled me a long hop outside off stump. Gratefully, I chopped it through the slips and I had done it."

While Hutton was hailed as a national hero by fans and press alike, one critic felt that he could have done just a bit better. "On the way from The Oval at the end of the game, I stopped at traffic lights," remembered Sir Len. "A woman in an adjoining car pulled down her window and said: 'Well done, Len, but why ever didn't you score one more run – one for each day of the year?' As I said to Denis [Compton] later: 'Denis, tell me, can you ever satisfy a woman?'"

Including Hutton's record innings, the ten highest individual Ashes scores are:

Year	Player	Venue	Score
1938	Len Hutton	The Oval	364
1930	Don Bradman	Headingley	334
1964	Bobby Simpson	Old Trafford	311
1966	Bob Cowper	Melbourne	307
1934	Don Bradman	Headingley	304
1903	Tip Foster	Sydney	287
1936/37	Don Bradman	Melbourne	270
1934	Bill Ponsford	The Oval	266
1964	Ken Barrington	Old Trafford	256
1930	Don Bradman	Lord's	254

— BOTH'S GREAT MOMENT —

In 2002 Channel Four broadcast a show, presented by former footballer Vinnie Jones, entitled *100 Great Sporting Moments*. Ian Botham's single-handed demolition of the Aussies in 1981 came fifth in the following top ten:

1. Steve Redgrave wins fifth consecutive Olympic gold medal, 2000
2. Germany 1 England 5, World Cup qualifier, 2001
3. England win the World Cup, 1966
4. Manchester United win the Champions League, 1999
5. Botham's Ashes, 1981
6. Diego Maradona's goals v England, 1986
7. Muhammed Ali v George Foreman, 'The Rumble in the Jungle', 1974
8. Jayne Torvill and Christopher Dean win gold, Winter Olympics 1984
9. Dennis Taylor wins World Snooker Championship on the final black, 1985
10. Bjorn Borg and John McEnroe play an epic tie-break at the Wimbledon men's final, 1980

Other Ashes moments to figure in the top 100 were Don Bradman's last Test innings against England in 1948 (number 87) and Shane Warne's 'ball of the century' to dismiss a bewildered Mike Gatting in 1993 (number 92).

— CAPTAINS' INNINGS —

Ashes matches in which both captains have scored centuries:

Year	Venue	Centurion skippers
1930	Lord's	Bill Woodfall (Aus) 155 and APF Chapman (Eng) 121
1938	Lord's	Wally Hammond (Eng) 240 and Don Bradman (Aus) 102*
1953	Lord's	Lindsay Hassett (Aus) 104 and Len Hutton (Eng) 145
1964	Old Trafford	Bobby Simpson (Aus) 311 and Ted Dexter (Eng) 174
1986/87	Adelaide	Mike Gatting (Eng) 100 and Allan Border (Aus) 100*
2005	Old Trafford	Michael Vaughan (Eng) 166 and Ricky Ponting (Aus) 156

— MEN OF THE MATCH 2005 —

Test	Venue	Man of the Match
First	Lord's	Glenn McGrath (Aus)
Second	Edgbaston	Andrew Flintoff (Eng)
Third	Old Trafford	Ricky Ponting (Aus)
Fourth	Trent Bridge	Andrew Flintoff (Eng)
Fifth	The Oval	Kevin Pietersen (Eng)

In addition to these awards, Andrew Flintoff (England) and Shane Warne (Australia) were voted as Men of the Series for their respective countries. Flintoff also picked up the inaugural Compton-Miller medal, named after former Ashes greats Denis Compton and Keith Miller, after being named player of the series.

— ELTON'S ASHES PARTY —

England retained the Ashes in Australia in 1986 thanks to an innings win in Melbourne just after Christmas. Among the celebrating England fans was singer Elton John who – never being one to miss out on a good party – headed straight for the tourists' hotel soon after the final Aussie wicket fell. As England's Gladstone Small later recalled, the players were delighted when Elton announced that he would be happy to play DJ for the night: "Beefy (Ian Botham) only had four CDs so we were pretty pleased when Elton turned up. He even sent his driver back to his hotel to pick up some more music. When he came back he had three suitcases full of CDs. Elton is a big cricket fan and was touring Australia, so he hung out with us whenever he could. Sometimes he would fly over to see us after a concert. As the celebrations wound down, I looked out of a window and saw people walking to work. What a night!"

— SUPER SKIPPERS —

No one has captained a side in more Ashes duels than former Aussie skipper Allan Border. The tough-as-nails batsman from Sydney led his team in 29 Tests (winning 13, losing six and drawing 10) between 1985 and 1993 before passing over the captaincy to Mark Taylor.

Allan Border (Aus) 29 Tests (1985–93)
Archie MacLaren (Eng) 20 Tests (1899–1909)
Joe Darling (Aus) 20 Tests (1899–1905)
Don Bradman (Aus) 19 Tests (1936–48)
Ricky Ponting (Aus) 19 Tests (2005–11)

— ASHES LEGENDS: DON BRADMAN —

Widely recognised as the greatest batsman ever, Don Bradman dominated the Ashes scene for two decades following his Test debut against England in 1928.

In his 20-year Test career 'The Don', as he was affectionately known, completely rewrote the record books. Perhaps the best indication of his run-making abilities is the fact that his Test average of 99.94 is 63% better than any other batsman who has played 20 or more innings. Indeed, but for a second-ball duck in his final Test innings against England in 1948 Bradman's average would have reached three figures.

That famous failure was very much out of character. No other Australian batsman has punished English bowlers to the extent that Bradman did. His total of 5,028 runs is an Ashes record which is unlikely to be surpassed. Nine hundred and seventy four of those runs came in the 1930 series, and included a personal best score of 334 at Headingley.

In the following Ashes series, England captain Douglas Jardine was so fearful of Bradman that he devised a controversial strategy, dubbed 'Bodyline' by the press, to counter the threat posed by the Australian batsman. Even so, Bradman still averaged well over 50 in the series – by his own high standards a comparative failure, but success by any other measure.

Bradman was appointed Australian captain for the 1936/37 series, and sensationally led his side to a 3–2 victory after they had trailed 2–0. Inevitably, 'The Don' played a central role in the comeback, notching scores of 270, 212 and 169 in consecutive Tests. He continued as captain after World War II, leading a powerful side known as 'The Invincibles' to a 4–0 series victory in England in 1948.

Bradman's ability to compile huge scores was based on a technique that was almost flawless. Strong on both sides of the wicket, The Don's superb stoke play stemmed from a combination of excellent vision, fast footwork and a decisive bat action which featured a powerful follow through. Comfortable against both fast and spin bowling, he was the original run-machine.

After retiring from cricket, Bradman worked as a stockbroker and cricket administrator, serving for nearly 30 years as a selector for the Australian team. He received a number of prestigious awards, including a knighthood in 1949 and the Companion of the Order of Australia (the country's highest civil honour) in 1979. A year before his death, aged 92 in 2001, he was unanimously selected by 100 experts as one of Wisden's five Cricketers of the Century. Naturally, however, it is in his native land that Bradman is revered most and, even to Aussies with little or no interest in cricket, he remains an iconic figure.

Don Bradman factfile
Born: Cootamundra, New South Wales, 27 August 1908
Died: 25 February 2001
State: New South Wales, South Australia
Ashes Tests: 37
Batting: 5,028 runs (ave 89.78)
Bowling: 1 wicket (ave 51.00)

Others on Bradman

"Bradman was a team in himself."
Jack Hobbs

"Bradman didn't break my heart in 1930, he just made me very, very tired."
England bowler **Harold Larwood**

'The Don'

— ASHES CLINCHING MOMENTS —

The runs and wickets that settled the destiny of the Ashes in England's favour:

- **1933, Brisbane:** England middle-order batsman Eddie Paynter, who was suffering from acute tonsillitis and had spent the Test commuting from his sick bed at Brisbane General Hospital (see *Beyond the Call of Duty*, page 102), gave England an unassailable 3–1 lead in the Bodyline series by clubbing Stan McCabe for six.

- **1953, The Oval:** England's 19-year quest for the Ashes came to an end when, after four draws in the previous Tests, Denis Compton swept the winning boundary down to The Oval gas holders giving the home side an eight-wicket victory.

- **1956, Old Trafford:** Jim Laker trapped Australian tail-ender Len Maddocks lbw to take his tenth wicket of the innings, rounding off a convincing England win that guaranteed the home side would retain the Ashes.

- **1971, Sydney:** At 12.36pm on the last day's play Keith Fletcher caught Terry Jenner off the bowling of Derek Underwood to wrap up a 2–0 series victory for England. Captain Ray Illingworth was chaired off the pitch by his team-mates as the tourists celebrated their first Ashes win over Australia for 15 years.

- **1981, Old Trafford:** Mike Gatting caught Mike Whitney off the bowling of Bob Willis to clinch a 103-run victory for England. The win also gave Mike Brearley's side a 3–1 lead with just a single Test to play, maintaining England's grip on the Ashes.

- **1986, Melbourne:** With Australia facing an innings defeat and on the verge of going 2–0 down in the penultimate Test, Merv Hughes attempted to swipe Phil Edmonds' delivery out of the ground but only succeeded in providing a straightforward catch for Gladstone Small in the deep. "It was an easy catch," recalled Small later. "There was no real pressure because we were so far ahead. As it landed in my hands I heard (Mike) Gatting's squeaky voice shout, 'Yeah, we've done it'. I threw the ball high into the air and ran around like a lunatic."

- **2005, The Oval:** The sight of umpires Billy Bowden and Rudi Koertzen emerging from The Oval pavilion to remove the bails one last time may not have been the most exciting moment of a thrilling summer's cricket, but it was still rapturously applauded by the English contingent in the crowd as it signalled that the match was a draw and, far more importantly, the end of Australia's 16-year stranglehold on the Ashes.

- **2009, The Oval:** Aussie middle-order batsman Mike Hussey had battled bravely to make a century but when he bat-padded Graeme Swann's delivery to Alastair Cook at short leg his long innings was over. More importantly, his dismissal meant that England had regained the Ashes with a 2–1 series win just two years after they had been humbled 5–0 Down Under.

— 'THE FINAL TEST' —

In 1953, the year England reclaimed the Ashes after a gap of 19 years, a film was released in which the ancient cricket clash between northern and southern hemispheres featured prominently. Directed by Anthony Asquith, *The Final Test* was based on a TV play by Terence Rattigan and starred Jack Warner, who was later to find fame as the eponymous policeman in *Dixon of Dock Green*. Warner played an England cricketer, Sam Palmer, who was making his last Test appearance of his career against Australia. Real-life Ashes cricketers Jim Laker, Alec Bedser, Godfrey Evans, Cyril Washbrook and Denis Compton made cameo appearances in the film, which largely focussed on the relationship between Palmer and his son, played by Ray Jackson.

Rather than watch his father slay the Aussie bowlers, the young Palmer chooses instead to visit a pompous poet played by Robert Morley. The poet, though, proves to be a cricket fanatic and ensures that father and son are reunited in a tear-jerking final scene. Bless.

— ASHES VENUES: AUSTRALIA —

The Melbourne Cricket Ground was the first ever venue for an England-Australia match, way back in 1877. Since then four other cities have got in on the act, the most recent being the WACA at Perth which gained Test status in 1970.

Over the years, England's preferred venue has been Sydney, possibly because of the number of ex-pats who have made it their home. Australia, though, still boast a better record at the Sydney Cricket Ground, as indeed they do at all the Test grounds Down Under.

Ground	Ashes debut	Ashes Tests	England wins	Australia wins	Draws
Melbourne	1877	54	20	27	7
Sydney	1882	54	22	25	7
Adelaide Oval	1884	30	9	16	5
Gabba, Brisbane*	1933	20	5	10	5
WACA, Perth	1970	12	1	8	3

* Includes one match at the Exhibition Ground, Brisbane (1928)

— AD BREAK —

Ashes stars who have appeared in UK television ads include:

Mike Atherton (Cricket Master, 1996)
Ian Botham (Shredded Wheat, 2000)
Ian Botham and Allan Lamb (English beef and lamb, 2005)
Andrew Flintoff (Morrisons, 2011)
Graham Gooch and Shane Warne (Advanced Hair Studios, 2005)
Darren Gough (Physio Sport, 2000)
Nasser Hussain (NPower, 2001)

— WHITEWASHED! —

Until the scoreline was equalled by Australia in 2006/07, the biggest series victory in Ashes history was way back in 1920/21 when the England touring party Down Under was hammered 5–0 in a five-match contest. The home side's star performers were batsman Herbie Collins who averaged nearly 62 in his nine innings, and leg spinner Arthur Mailey who took 39 wickets in the series to set a new record for an Australian bowler in the Ashes. Mailey's impressive haul included nine wickets in England's second innings at the Melbourne Test, another record for an Aussie bowler.

Despite the presence of such famous names as Jack Hobbs, Frank Woolley and Wilfred Rhodes in their ranks, England were no match for their opponents and went down to some heavy defeats during the whitewash:

Test	Venue	Result
First	Sydney	Australia won by 377 runs
Second	Melbourne	Australia won by an innings and 91 runs
Third	Adelaide	Australia won by 119 runs
Fourth	Melbourne	Australia won by 8 wickets
Fifth	Sydney	Australia won by 9 wickets

As if to prove this rout was no fluke, Australia retained the Ashes with a 3–0 win in England in a three-match series in 1921. The Aussies also won all three Tests on home soil in 1979/80 (although the Ashes were not at stake on this occasion), while you have to go back to 1886 to find the only time England managed to win three out of three Tests against their oldest rivals. Over 40 years later, on the Australian tour of 1928/29, England had a great chance to complete a five-Test whitewash after winning their first four clashes against the old enemy. However, Percy Chapman's side went down to a five-wicket defeat in the final Test in Melbourne despite posting a total in excess of 500 in the first innings. (See *Whitewashed Again!*, page 89)

– ASHES 2010/11: THE STATS –

As you'd expect, England's convincing win Down Under in 2010/11 was reflected by the visitors' marked superiority in the key stats from the series:

	England	Australia
Runs	2,864	2,631
Highest innings score	644	481
Run rate/over	3.5	3.1
Runs/per wicket	51.1	29.2
Wickets lost	56	90
Centuries	9*	3
50s	10	16
Century partnerships	11	4
Ducks	6	10
Balls per wicket taken	56	88
Bowler taking five wickets in an innings	3	4
Catches	62	33
Run outs	3	0
No balls bowled	13	21

* Including two double centuries

— ASHES LEGENDS: FRED TRUEMAN —

A fast bowler with a classical sideways action, a mop of unruly black hair and an intimidating scowl, Fred Trueman was the first player in Test history to pass the 300-wicket mark.

Although just five feet ten, Trueman made the most of his wide shoulders and strong legs to generate genuine pace. At his peak, he was a frightening prospect for any batsman, living up to his 'Fiery Fred' nickname not only with the speed of his deliveries but also with the sharpness of his tongue. As Trueman later admitted, his outspokenness did not always go down with the selectors, who left him out of the England side on a number of occasions to the bewilderment of his many fans. "Some of the selectors did not like my forthright attitude, which they interpreted as being 'bolshy'," he said once. "Rather than pick the best 11 players for the job, the selection committee would often choose someone because he was, in their eyes, a gentleman and a decent chap."

A thorn in the side of the Australians for many years, often in tandem with Lancashire bowler Brian Statham, Trueman enjoyed his greatest day against the old enemy on his home ground of Headingley in 1961. After collecting five wickets in the first innings, he went one better in the second, at one stage taking five wickets for no runs while bowling off cutters.

After retiring from first-class cricket in 1968, Trueman went on to become a regular on *Test Match Special* for over a quarter of a century, his gruff Yorkshire delivery neatly complementing the more flamboyant style of some of his co-commentators. In the 1970s he also presented a TV programme called *Indoor League*, an unlikely celebration of northern pub life featuring 'sports' such as darts, skittles and arm wrestling.

'Fiery Fred'

Fred Trueman factfile
Born: Stainton, Yorkshire, 6 February 1931
Died: 1 July 2006
County: Yorkshire
Ashes Tests: 19 (1953–64)
Batting: 338 runs (ave 12.07)
Bowling: 77 wickets (ave 25.96)

Others on Trueman

"Without rival, the ripest, the richest, the rip-roaringest individual performer on cricket's stage."
AA Thomson in *The Cricketer*, 1961

"Fred not only bowled fast. He was a fast bowler to the very depths of his soul."
England and Yorkshire batsman **John Hampshire**

— WHAT A COMEBACK! —

On only one occasion in Ashes history has a team come back from two Tests down to win the series. The remarkable turnaround occurred in 1936/37 in Australia, Don Bradman's first series as Aussie captain.

England dominated the First Test at Brisbane, winning by 322 runs thanks in part to a 10-wicket haul by Bill Voce, one of the leading figures in the controversial Bodyline series four years earlier. The tourists' good form continued in the Second Test at Sydney, where an unbeaten double century by Wally Hammond was a key factor in England's victory by an innings and 22 runs.

The Ashes, held by Australia following their series victory in 1934, appeared to be heading back to England but the home side were determined to clutch on to the famous urn. In the Third Test at Melbourne the Australians finally got into their stride, Bradman (270) and Jack Fingleton (136) sharing an Ashes record sixth wicket partnership of 346 as England went down to a 365-run defeat. The Fourth Test at Adelaide was closer, but another double century by 'The Don' paved the way for a second Aussie win.

The momentum was now with the home side and they rammed home their advantage in the Fifth and final Test at Melbourne, centuries by Bradman, Stan McCabe and Jack Badcock contributing to an impressive first innings total of 604. England, who looked to have had the Ashes sewn up just weeks earlier, had no reply and lost by an innings.

Against the odds, the Aussies had pulled off one of the most unlikely series wins in the long and distinguished history of the Ashes.

— PROPERLY PACKERED! —

The 1978/79 series in Australia was a memorable one for Mike Brearley's England side, the tourists thrashing the Aussies 5–1 to record their most emphatic victory ever in the Ashes.

In their defence, the Australians were severely hampered by mass defections to Kerry Packer's rebel World Series Cricket, depriving them of virtually a whole 'First XI' including household names such as the Chappell brothers, fast bowler Dennis Lillee and wicketkeeper Rodney Marsh. Nonetheless, England could rightly claim that they could only beat the side picked to play against them, and that's precisely what they proceeded to do.

Australia's weakened team got off to a poor start in the First Test at Brisbane, making just 116 in their first innings with the England quicks Bob Willis, Chris Old and Ian Botham doing the damage. The home side fared better second time round, centuries from skipper Graham Yallop and Kim Hughes helping them past 300, but England still strolled to victory by seven wickets.

The visitors won equally comfortably in Perth in the Second Test, a century by David Gower helping England record a useful first innings total before the Australians were twice bowled out cheaply to slump to defeat by 166 runs.

It was a different story in Melbourne, though. Most of the new players promoted to the Australian team had seemed lacking in confidence and quality, but that accusation could not be levelled at pace bowler Rodney Hogg, who would eventually claim 41 wickets in the series to become the one genuine home success story of an otherwise dismal campaign. He had already impressed with some fiery and aggressive spells in the previous Tests, and in a low-scoring contest took 10 wickets in the match as the Aussies won by 103 runs.

In the Fourth Test in Sydney, too, Australia were on top in the opening stages, taking a formidable first innings lead. With the series, and their hold on the Ashes, in the balance, England were indebted to Derek Randall, who hit a magnificent 150 out of the tourists' second innings total of 346. Set 204 to win, Australia failed dismally, making just 111 with England spinners Geoff Miller and John Emburey bagging seven wickets between them.

The fate of the Ashes decided, the teams moved on to Adelaide for the Fifth Test, where Australia gave themselves a chance by bowling England out for just 169. However, the Aussies' feeble batting was again exposed as they posted just 164 in reply. England were struggling in their second innings until an unlikely seventh-wicket stand of 135 between Miller and wicketkeeper Bob Taylor revived their fortunes, and they eventually set Australia a target of 366. Once more the Aussies failed to cope with the English attack's mix of spin and seam, and they went down to another heavy defeat.

By this stage, the end of the series couldn't come soon enough for the demoralised Aussies. At least skipper Yallop showed some fighting spirit in the Sixth Test at Sydney, scoring a superb 121 – unfortunately, the rest of his team-mates managed just another 77 runs between them. Trailing England by 110, Australia were dismissed for a paltry 143 in their second innings – incredibly, the ninth time in 12 attempts that the home side had failed to pass 200 – and the tourists romped home to victory by nine wickets.

The 1978/79 Ashes had been a triumph for England and a catastrophe for Australia, whatever excuses they might proffer regarding their missing stars. For Aussie captain Yallop, too, the series was a personal disaster as he later admitted, writing: "My name is now eternally entrenched in the record books as the man who led his country to that ignominious hiding against England."

— TOP CAPS —

Australia's Syd Gregory has played in more Ashes Tests than any other player, having taken the field against England on 52 occasions between 1890 and 1912. For England, former skipper Colin Cowdrey leads the way with 43 appearances between 1954 and 1975, when he was dramatically recalled to the team for the winter's tour Down Under one month short of his 42nd birthday. Including this illustrious pair, the ten most capped Ashes cricketers are:

Player	Ashes caps
Syd Gregory (Aus, 1890–1912)	52
Allan Border (Aus, 1978–93)	47
Colin Cowdrey (Eng, 1954–75)	43
Warwick Armstrong (Aus, 1902–21)	42
Graham Gooch (Eng, 1975–95)	42
David Gower (Eng, 1978–91)	42
Rodney Marsh (Aus, 1970–83)	42
Clem Hill (Aus, 1896–1912)	41
Jack Hobbs (Eng, 1908–30)	41
Wilfred Rhodes (Eng, 1899–1926)	41

— PEEL'S PAIRS —

England left-arm spinner Robert 'Bobby' Peel holds the unfortunate distinction of being the only cricketer to have been dismissed for three pairs in Ashes matches. Peel failed to trouble the scorers in either innings of the Third Test in Adelaide in 1894/95 and followed up that failure by twice being stumped for a big round zero in the Fourth Test at Sydney – making him the first player in Test history to be dismissed without scoring in four consecutive innings.

Two years later at The Oval Peel collected another pair against the Aussies, but at least he had the last laugh on this occasion as his six-wicket haul in Australia's second innings was a crucial factor in England's 66-run victory.

— BORN ABROAD ENGLAND ASHES XI —

Here's a team of players who represented England against Australia despite being born outside the United Kingdom:

1. Graeme Hick (Zimbabwe)
2. Ted Dexter (Italy)
3. Colin Cowdrey (India)
4. Kevin Pietersen (South Africa)
5. Derek Pringle (Kenya)
6. Geraint Jones (Papua New Guinea)
7. Freddy Brown (Peru)
8. Phil Edmonds (Zambia)
9. George 'Gubby' Allen (Australia)
10. Gladstone Small (Barbados)
11. Devon Malcolm (Jamaica)

— THE 'OTHER' CENTENARY TESTS —

Since the famous Centenary Test in 1977, Australia and England have played two other one-off Tests to celebrate significant anniversaries.

The first occasion, at Lord's in 1980, marked the centenary of the first ever Test match played in England – a five-wicket victory for the home side against the visiting Aussies at The Oval. To the disappointment of the fans, the event was badly affected by rain and took a while to get going, Australia batting on until the third day before declaring on 385–5, a total built on centuries by both Graeme Wood and Kim Hughes. The contest livened up when England were dismissed for just 205, Aussie pace bowler Len Pascoe taking five wickets. The visitors rammed home their advantage by scoring a quickfire 189–4 in the second innings, before declaring to set England 370 to win on the final day. Ian Botham's side, though, never looked in trouble and, aided by an unbeaten century from opener Geoff Boycott, were able to bat out the match for a draw.

Eight years later, in 1988, the two sides met again in Sydney in a single Test to commemorate the bicentenary of permanent white settlement in Australia. Batting first, England made a useful score of 425, Chris Broad top scoring with 139. The opener, though, blotted his copybook when he was bowled by Steve Waugh, angrily smashing the stumps with his bat – an action which saw him fined £500. Australia performed poorly in reply, and were forced to follow on 211 runs in arrears. An England victory looked to be on the cards, but Aussie opener David Boon had other ideas, scoring an unbeaten 184 to guide his team to a comfortable draw.

— MAROONED ON 99 —

Imagine batting to within one run of an Ashes century and then watching helplessly as your team's last wicket falls. Well, that's exactly what happened to Geoff Boycott at Perth in 1979/80 – the first time in Test history that a batsman had been left high and dry on 99. Boycott, who some claimed was more interested in his own success than that of the team, was left fuming after last man Bob Willis got out for 0 in England's second innings.

Six years later against England in Perth, Steve Waugh experienced an identical fate when he was stranded one short of his century after a mix-up with his brother Mark, who was acting as a runner, resulted in Craig McDermott being run out.

Meanwhile, the following players have endured the heartbreak of being dismissed just one run short of an Ashes century:

Year	Player	Venue
1902	Clem Hill (Aus)	Melbourne
1912	Charlie Macartney (Aus)	Lord's
1934	Arthur Chipperfield (Aus)	Trent Bridge
1938	Eddie Paynter (Eng)	Lord's
1951	Keith Miller (Aus)	Adelaide
1962	Ted Dexter (Eng)	Brisbane
1965	Bob Cowper (Aus)	Melbourne
1975	Ross Edwards (Aus)	Lord's
1993	Mark Waugh (Aus)	Lord's
1993	Mike Atherton (Eng)	Lord's

— ARE YOU SURE, UMPIRE? —

Virtually every Ashes series has had its fair share of controversial umpiring decisions. Here's a selection of some of some of the incidents which had one side up in arms and the other heaving a collective sigh of relief:

- **Darling's reprieve, Sydney, 1898**
  Australia had already reclaimed the Ashes by the time of the Fifth Test, but nonetheless the match was as competitive as ever. The home side were chasing 275 to win, when the Aussies' star batsman, Joe Darling, appeared to be plum lbw. A huge appeal went up from the England players but umpire Charles Bannerman, a former Australian Test cricketer, failed to raise his finger, claiming he was unsighted by the bowler running across his line of vision. England wicketkeeper Bill Storer accused Bannerman of cheating and was later severely rebuked. Darling's reprieve proved crucial as he went on from 50 to make a match-winning 160.

- **Bradman's lucky break, Brisbane, 1946**
  England were sure they had captured the prize wicket of 'The Don' for just 28 when he sliced a Bill Voce delivery to Jack Ikin at second slip. However, the umpire turned down the appeal, suggesting that the ball had hit the ground before being caught. Bradman went on to make 187, and Australia won the match by an innings. Afterwards, England captain Wally Hammond told Bradman, "I thought it was a catch, but I may have been wrong." Whether the decision was right or wrong, it certainly cost England dear.

- **Aussie umpires' lbw phobia, 1970/71**
  Remarkably, during this six-match Ashes series Down Under the three home umpires, messrs Brooks, Rowan and O'Connell, failed to give a single Australian batsman out lbw. Even more remarkably, England (who were on the wrong end of five lbw decisions during the series) still managed to win back the Ashes with a 2–0 victory.

- **Allan Lamb's boot, Edgbaston, 1985**
  With the series poised at 1–1, Australia were fighting for a draw when Wayne Phillips hammered a ball from England spinner Phil Edmonds onto the boot of Allan Lamb, fielding at silly point. The ball bounced up, David Gower took the catch and umpire David Shepherd raised his finger. After their innings defeat, the Aussies disputed the decision, claiming that Shepherd could not have been sure that the ball did not also touch the ground while hitting Lamb. "I considered it rough justice indeed," fumed

skipper Allan Border. "I've relived this incident a hundred times since and wondered what might have been had Phillips survived that appeal."

- **Dean Headley 'runs out' Michael Slater, Sydney, 1998/99**
  After England fielder Dean Headley scored a direct hit on the stumps, Aussie opener Michael Slater seemed resigned to his fate, taking off his gloves. But umpire Steve Dunn, from New Zealand, was unsure what decision to make and referred the verdict to the third umpire, Simon Taufel. Unfortunately for England, however, the TV footage was little help as the stumps were obscured by bowler Peter Such. Slater was given 'not out' and went on to make a match-winning century.

- **Steve Harmison seals victory, Edgbaston, 2005**
  Australia needed just three runs for victory when tailender Michael Kasprowicz gloved a delivery from Harmison through to wicketkeeper Geraint Jones. Yet, as the England players embraced in a victory huddle, TV replays showed that Kasprowicz's hand was not on his bat when the ball hit his glove – so, technically, he was not out. To be fair, the Aussies didn't make too much of the incident, although Kasprowicz was heard to mutter, "I will be leaving with the most vivid delivery that I will replay over in my mind for the rest of my life."

— FOLLOW ON SUCCESS —

Incredibly, England have twice beaten Australia after following on in their second innings.

England first pulled off this conjuror's trick in a timeless Test in Sydney in 1894. Batting first, Australia compiled the impressive total of 586, with George Giffen and Syd Gregory scoring 161 and 201 respectively. After making just 325 in reply, England were asked to follow on by Australian skipper Jack Blackham. Second time around, the visitors made a better fist of things, opener Albert Ward hitting a century and a number of other batsmen making useful contributions as England were all out for 437. This left Australia requiring 177 to win and, at the close of play on the fifth day with the home side on 113–2, a comfortable victory appeared in sight. By the time the Aussies had advanced to 130–2 on the morning of the sixth day, the match appeared all but over, but thanks to some inspired bowling by left arm spinners Bobby Peel (6–67) and Johnny Briggs (3–25) England managed to capture the last eight Australian wickets for just 36 runs to record a famous victory by the slender margin of ten runs.

In 1981 England again pulled off an unlikely win after following on, this time in even more dramatic circumstances. Trailing by 227 runs after the first innings, the match seemed destined for an early finish when England slumped to 135–7 in their second knock. At this point, though, Ian Botham began flaying the Aussie bowlers around the field and, supported by tailenders Graham Dilley, Chris Old and Bob Willis, took England's total to a respectable 356, Botham contributing an unbeaten 149 which included 27 fours and a six. The home side's lead, however, was still only 129, a target which looked well within Australia's reach, especially once they had advanced to 56–1. But the game was to swiftly change course again as fast bowler Bob Willis, bowling with real venom despite having almost missed the match with a chest infection, ripped through the Australian order. At 75–8 England took on the mantle of favourites for the first time in the Test, only for a dogged stand of 35 between Ray Bright and Dennis Lillee to swing the match back Australia's way. Summoning up the last of his energy supplies, though, Willis dismissed both batsman to give England a memorable victory by just 18 runs. (See *Quids in at Headingley*, page 151)

— BEFUDDLED BY WARNE —

Few would dispute that Shane Warne was the star performer for Australia during the 2005 Ashes series. His 40 wickets in the five Tests took his Ashes total to a record 172 and confirmed his status as one of the greatest bowlers of all-time.

All of England's batsmen, with the possible exception of Kevin Pietersen, found Warne a real handful, but Andrew Strauss and Ashley Giles were especially vulnerable to the spin master. Warne dismissed both players an incredible six times during the series, while conceding an average of just 20.83 runs to Strauss and a paltry 5.67 runs to Giles. For good measure, Warne also dismissed Marcus Trescothick five times during the series, at a cost of only 16.80 runs on average.

— MILLER SAVES THE DAY —

Before the heart-thumping drama of Edgbaston 2005, the closest Ashes encounter in living memory was the Fourth Test at Melbourne in 1982.

Three runs behind after the first innings, England were all out for 294 second time around, meaning that Australia needed to score 292 to take a decisive 3–0 lead in the series. When the Aussies were reduced to 218–9, England pace bowler Norman Cowans having taken six of the wickets to fall, the home side's chances of victory appeared slight. By the close of play on the fourth day, however, a defiant last wicket stand between middle-order batsman Allan Border and tailender Jeff Thomson had advanced the score to 255–9. If not exactly in sight, an unlikely Australian win could not be entirely ruled out.

The next morning 18,000 noisy fans gained free entry to the ground, the majority of them hoping that Border and Thomson could pull off a great escape. Once play started the pair continued to chip away at their target, Border protecting Thomson as much as possible by claiming the bulk of the strike. Soon the runs required were down to single figures, and still the English bowlers couldn't find a breakthrough. Almost in desperation, England captain Bob Willis threw the ball to Ian Botham, a bowler who could either be lethal or waywardly expensive, depending on his mood. Happily for England, Botham produced a snorter with his first delivery, Thomson dabbed nervously at the ball and it flew to Chris Tavaré at second slip. Normally, the Kent batsman was a reliable slip fielder, but he boobed big time on this occasion, the ball slipping from his grasp. Fortunately for Tav, though, Geoff Miller at first slip reacted quickly, and stooping low, managed to pouch the ball before it hit the deck. In an unforgettable climax, England had won by just three runs.

— NO FOLLOW ON —

After Australia dismissed England for 157 in reply to their 602–9 declared in the First Test at Brisbane in 2006, most of those watching expected Aussie captain Ricky Ponting to invite the tourists to bat again. Instead, he opted to send out his own pair of openers to create a new Test match record for the largest first innings lead (445 runs) after which the follow on has not been enforced. Ultimately, Ponting's decision made little difference to the outcome, as Australia still won the match by the comfortable margin of 277 runs.

— CARRYING HIS BAT —

The following openers batted throughout a completed Ashes innings, remaining not out at the fall of the last wicket:

Player	Year	Venue	Score	Team total
Jack Barrett (Aus)	1890	Lord's	67*	176
Bobby Abel (Eng)	1892	Sydney	132*	307
Warren Bardsley (Aus)	1926	Lord's	193*	383
Bill Woodfull (Aus)	1928	Brisbane	30*	66
Bill Woodfull (Aus)	1933	Adelaide	73*	193
Bill Brown (Aus)	1938	Lord's	206*	422
Len Hutton (Eng)	1951	Adelaide	156*	272
Bill Lawry (Aus)	1971	Sydney	60*	116
Geoff Boycott (Eng)	1979	Perth	99*	215

* not out

— ASHES LEGENDS: FRANK TYSON —

Frank Tyson's reputation rests largely on his performances in the 1954/55 Ashes tour, where his fiery bowling earned him the nickname 'Typhoon Tyson' and his 28 Test wickets were instrumental in England's success.

The series, though, began disastrously for Tyson, whose single wicket cost him 160 runs in the opening Test in Brisbane. At Sydney in the Second Test, however, Tyson was transformed. Bowling off a shortened run he added accuracy to his raw pace and, after surviving a nasty scare when he was knocked unconscious by a Ray Lindwall bouncer, he took ten wickets in the match as England turned around a first innings deficit to win by 38 runs. In the following Test at Melbourne, Tyson produced the fastest and most productive spell of his career, taking 7–27 in the second innings as England again came from behind to win. "This was intelligence, rhythm and strength merged into the violent craft of fast bowling," wrote John Arlott of Tyson's match-winning display. Thanks largely to the efforts of the former Durham University student, England went on to win the series 3–1, retaining the Ashes they won in 1953.

Although Tyson appeared in two more Ashes series, injuries and his energy-sapping action took their toll and the 'Typhoon' of Melbourne was never seen again. He retired from cricket aged 30, shortly after emigrating to Australia. He later became coach of Victoria, and occasionally appeared on television as a commentator.

Frank Tyson factfile
Born: Farnworth, Lancashire, 6 June 1930
County: Northants
Ashes Tests: 8 (1954–59)
Batting: 117 runs (ave 9.00)
Bowling: 32 wickets (ave 25.31)

Others on Tyson

"He is intelligent beyond the usual run of fast bowlers: he is the type of cricketer who improves rapidly through thinking about the game."
Cricket writer **John Arlott**, 1956

"For a short time, Frank Tyson blasted all-comers."
Richie Benaud

— ALL OF A TWITTER —

If you want to know what Andrew Flintoff's drinking or who Shane Warne's dating then you can get the latest gossip straight from the horse's mouth on Twitter. Here's a list of some of the former and current Ashes stars you can find tweeting their latest thoughts on the trendy social networking site:

Player	Followers
Shane Warne (Warne888)	416,574
Andrew Flintoff (flintoff11)	240,579
Graeme Swann (Swannyg66)	207,889
Jimmy Anderson (JimmyAnderson9)	159,684
Michael Clarke (MClarke23)	116,639
Tim Bresnan (timbresnan)	65,015

— LOST AT LORD'S —

Northants' middle-order batsman David Steele was a surprise call-up by England for the Second Test at Lord's in 1975, the 33-year-old having spent a dozen summers in the county game without ever getting near the national team.

Grey-haired and bespectacled, Steele didn't exactly look like an international sportsman and the doubts surrounding his selection only increased when he failed to appear from the Lord's pavilion following the fall of England's first wicket. Some fans must have wondered whether Steele, concerned at the prospect of facing of Australia's fearsome strike bowlers Dennis Lillee and Jeff Thompson, had simply lost his nerve and was still cowering in the dressing room. They would have been well wide of the mark, as Steele himself later explained: "I went down one flight of stairs too many – but I got to the crease eventually." Nonetheless, his delayed appearance meant that Steele only narrowly avoided becoming the first batsman in Test cricket to be timed out.

Once out at the wicket, however, the gritty right-hander put his inauspicious start behind him, battling his way to 50 and helping England recover from a poor opening session to draw the match. Famously dubbed 'the bank clerk who went to war' by *The Sun* newspaper, Steele scored a further three 50s in the four-Test series and, although he couldn't prevent Australia retaining the Ashes, he became an unlikely hero for English cricket followers and the wider public, who voted him BBC Sports Personality of the Year for 1975.

— THRASHED! —

The Ashes series has seen some remarkably close-fought battles over the years, but also some very one-sided contests. None more so than the 1938 Test at The Oval which England, thanks in no small part to Len Hutton's famous knock of 364, won by the staggering margin of an innings and 579 runs – a world record for Test match cricket.

By comparison, Australia's record win against England (see list below) seems like an edge-of-the-seat affair . . .

Year	Venue	Result
1938	The Oval	England beat Australia by an innings and 579 runs
1946	Brisbane	Australia beat England by an innings and 332 runs
1892	Adelaide	England beat Australia by an innings and 230 runs
1912	Melbourne	England beat Australia by an innings and 225 runs
1886	The Oval	England beat Australia by an innings and 217 runs

In the 2010/11 series in Australia Andrew Strauss's England side won three of the five matches by an innings, the first such hat-trick by a touring team in the history of Test cricket. Although none of the tourists' victories were sufficiently emphatic to make the above list, they were nonetheless utterly convincing triumphs, topped by the innings and 157-run win in Melbourne in the Fourth Test.

— FLYING START XI —

A team of England and Australia players who all scored a century in their very first innings against the old enemy:

1. WG Grace (Eng), 152 at The Oval, 1880
2. Kepler Wessels (Aus), 162 at Brisbane, 1982
3. Bill Ponsford (Aus), 110 at Sydney, 1924
4. Greg Chappell (Aus), 108 at Perth, 1970
5. Tip Foster (Eng), 287 at Sydney, 1903
6. Mark Waugh (Aus), 138 at Adelaide, 1991
7. Nawab of Pataudi (Eng), 102 at Sydney, 1932
8. Doug Walters (Aus), 155 at Brisbane, 1965
9. George Gunn (Eng), 119 Sydney, 1907
10. Charles Bannerman (Aus), 165* at Melbourne, 1877
11. Harry Graham (Aus), 107 at Lord's, 1893
* not out

— DOUBLE ENGLAND SKIPPERS —

Two players have captained England at cricket against Australia and also skippered their country at rugby. The first of these sporting all-rounders was Albert Hornby, the England cricket captain who lost the one-off Oval Test against the Aussies in 1882 which gave rise to the Ashes series. Universally known as 'Monkey' Hornby, thanks to his short stature and excessive energy, he also captained England at rugby in the same year.

Andrew Stoddart is the only other player to have captained England in both sports. As well as featuring in ten rugby internationals, Stoddart took on coin-tossing duties for England in eight Tests, including the 1894/95 series against the Australians. England's 3–2 series victory on this tour led the magazine *Punch* to celebrate the triumph with a poem which contained the following lines:

> "Then wrote the Queen of England
> Whose hand is blessed by God
> I must do something handsome
> For my dear victorious Stod"

— STAMP OF VICTORY —

In October 2005 the Royal Mail issued four stamps commemorating England's Ashes triumph earlier that year. The two first-class stamps and two 68p ones featured images of England players, including skipper Michael Vaughan, all-rounder Andrew Flintoff and star batsman Kevin Pietersen.

The issue broke with tradition, being the first time that living people other than members of the Royal Family could clearly be identified on a set of stamps. Launching the issue, Julietta Edgar, Head of Special Stamps at the Royal Mail, said: "England's victory in this summer's Ashes series certainly counts as a momentous occasion, making it an ideal topic for a set of Royal Mail special stamps. I'm sure the public will love using these stamps every day to continue the legacy of this sporting achievement."

The 68p stamps proved especially popular . . . possibly because they exactly matched the cost of sending a gloating postcard Down Under.

— JIM HAS AUSSIES IN A SPIN —

England off-spin bowler Jim Laker holds the record for the most dismissals in an Ashes match with an incredible 19 wickets in the Old Trafford Test of 1956. In the first innings Laker took 9–37, only being denied a clean sweep when fellow spinner and Surrey colleague Tony Lock took the third Aussie wicket to fall, Colin Cowdrey catching opener Jim Burke. In the second innings Laker went one better, grabbing all ten Aussie wickets for 53 runs to give him amazing match figures of 19–90.

When Laker arrived home after his record-breaking display, his wife, who was from Austria and knew very little about cricket, greeted him with the words, "Jim, did you do something good today?" She was puzzled after spending much of the afternoon answering congratulatory phone calls.

Australia's best match bowling figures are held by Bob Massie, who took eight wickets in each of England's innings on his Test debut at Lord's in 1972. "People are surprised when I tell them the wicket we played on in that game was actually quite good," the swing bowler said later. "It didn't do much off the wicket, but it swung in the air all right."

Most wickets in a match

Year	Player	Venue	Wickets	Runs	1st Innings	2nd Innings
1956	Jim Laker	Old Trafford	19	90	9–37	10–53
1972	Bob Massie	Lord's	16	137	8–84	8–53
1934	Hedley Verity	Lord's	15	104	7–61	8–43
1904	Wilfred Rhodes	Melbourne	15	124	7–56	8–68
1882	Fred Spofforth	The Oval	14	90	7–46	7–44
1953	Alec Bedser	Trent Bridge	14	99	7–55	7–44
1883	Billy Bates	Melbourne	14	102	7–28	7–74

*Spin king
Jim Laker*

— ASHES LEGENDS: RICHIE BENAUD —

Familiar to cricket lovers the world over as the sport's premier commentator, Richie Benaud first rose to fame as an all-rounder in the Australian side of the 1950s.

One of the most revered and influential leg spinners in the history of the game, Benaud developed his bowling skills under the watchful eye of his father – himself a first grade cricketer who on one occasion took all 20 wickets in a match. Like his great fan Shane Warne, Benaud had a huge variety of deliveries with which he could bamboozle the opposition, including the googly, the top-spinner and the flipper. He was also a decent lower-order batsman and a superb fielder, especially close to the wicket.

After some steady but hardly eye-catching performances for his country in the mid-1950s, Benaud emerged as a top-class all-rounder on the 1957/58 tour of South Africa. The following year he was, somewhat surprisingly, appointed Australia captain for the visit of Ashes holders England. Benaud proved to be an inspirational skipper, while his personal haul of 31 wickets in the series was a major factor in his side's emphatic 4–0 victory. Under Benaud, Australia retained the Ashes in a further two series before a longstanding shoulder injury prompted his retirement from the game.

Richie Benaud

Taking up cricket journalism and commentary, Benaud proved to be a natural broadcaster. As a captain he was cool, analytical, communicative and authoritative; on television, where he worked for the BBC, Channel 4 and Channel Nine in Australia, he was very much the same. Never ruffled and always informative, Benaud also developed a number of much-imitated catchphrases, including 'Good morning, everyone', 'Marvellous!' and 'Got 'im', all delivered in his distinctive Aussie twang. Benaud commentated on his last Test in England during the Ashes series at the Oval in 2005. Typically, the consummate pro signed off in deadpan style, simply saying, "McGrath got his man, and up in the commentary box now, Mark Nicholas and Tony Greig."

Richie Benaud factfile
Born: Penrith, New South Wales, 6 October 1930
State: New South Wales
Ashes Tests: 27 (1953–63)
Batting: 767 runs (ave 19.67)
Bowling: 83 wickets (ave 31.82)

Others on Benaud

"I saw Richie Benaud bowl as a kid and I was fascinated by him."
Shane Warne

"He planned every move from the time he got up in the morning to the time he went to bed."
Former Australian team-mate **Bobby Simpson** on Benaud's captaincy

— FAMILIAR ENDING TO CENTENARY TEST —

In March 1977 England played a one-off Test against Australia to mark the 100th anniversary of the first meeting between the two sides in Melbourne. Again Melbourne was the venue and again, incredibly, Australia won by the same 45-run margin as they had done a century earlier.

Yet an Australian victory had appeared unlikely after England captain Tony Greig put the home side in to bat and then watched as his bowlers skittled out the old enemy for just 138 runs. England, though, fared even worse, Dennis Lillee (6–26) and Max Walker (4–54) sharing the wickets as the visitors were dismissed for 95.

With the wicket easing, the batsmen got on top in the second innings. Rodney Marsh became the first Australian wicketkeeper to hit a century against England as the Aussies declared on 419–9. Set 463 to win, England came close thanks to a superb 174 from Derek Randall. But, as in Melbourne all those years ago, not quite close enough.

— FREDDIE'S ICE CREAM TRIBUTE —

Among the more bizarre tributes to the victorious England Ashes side of 2005 was the creation of two new ice creams in the team's honour.

The pair of vanilla-based ice creams were the work of Elaine Silverdell, the owner of Silverdell's ice cream parlour and bookshop in Kirkham, near Preston. One ice cream, Ashes 2005, was embedded with chocolate candy dust to symbolise the mythical ashes; the other, Freddie's Glory, acknowledged the immense contribution of local hero Andrew Flintoff to England's triumph and featured a St. George's cross motif.

— FREE RUNS —

The most extras – or 'sundries', as the Aussies prefer to call them – conceded in a single Ashes innings is 61 by England's bowlers in Australia's total of 602–6 declared at Trent Bridge in 1989. The figure was made up of six byes, 23 leg byes, three wides and 29 no-balls. The England bowlers' generosity helped the Aussies win the match by the convincing margin of an innings and 180 runs.

— THE GREAT ASHES SERIES: 'ILLY'S TRIUMPH', AUSTRALIA 1970/71 —

In search of their first Ashes triumph since 1956, Ray Illingworth's England, which included such famous names as Geoff Boycott, John Edrich, Basil D'Oliveira and John Snow, looked well equipped to give the Aussies a run for their money. Some critics, though, wondered whether an ageing squad, dubbed 'Dad's Army', would stand up to the rigours of a long tour. For their part, Bill Lawry's Aussies were confident that their mix of old stagers and young guns like the Chappell brothers, Ian and Greg, fast bowler Dennis Lillee and wicketkeeper Rodney Marsh could keep the tourists at bay.

The series took a while to get going, with two high-scoring draws in the first two Tests. Following a wash-out at Melbourne, England dominated the Fourth Test at Sydney from start to finish and, with paceman Snow taking 7–40 in the Aussies' second innings, won by 299 runs.

A hastily arranged Test at Melbourne finished in another tame draw, Ian Chappell's century for the home side being cancelled out by tons for England opener Brian Luckhurst and D'Oliveira.

In Adelaide, Illingworth surprisingly decided not to enforce the follow on when he had the chance and, thanks to second innings centuries by Ian Chappell and Keith Stackpole, the Australians escaped with a draw to set up an Ashes decider in Sydney.

The match proved to be the most dramatic of the series. After being dismissed cheaply, England responded with a hail of bouncers from Snow. When one hit Aussie tailender Terry Jenner on the head and forced him to seek hospital treatment the crowd reacted angrily, pelting Snow with empty beer cans as he took up his fielding position at fine leg. Illingworth promptly led his team from the field in protest, but the England players swiftly returned when the umpires warned that any further delay would see them award the match – and the Ashes – to the Australians.

Having trailed by 80 runs on the first innings, England's batsmen set their opponents 223 to win the Test. The target appeared eminently achievable but a fine all-round bowling effort by England saw the Aussies crumble to 160 all out.

When it came to the crunch, the visitors had held their nerve under pressure and Illingworth's men fully deserved their 2–0 series win. Captain Mainwearing and co. would have been proud of them.

First Test: Brisbane, Nov 27–Dec 2
Australia 433 & 214, England 464 & 39–1
Match drawn

Second Test: Perth, Dec 11–16
England 397 & 287–6 dec, Australia 440 & 100–3
Match drawn

Third Test: Melbourne, Dec 31–Jan 5
Match abandoned on the third day without a ball being bowled

Fourth Test: Sydney, Jan 9–14
England 332 & 319–5 dec, Australia 236 & 116
England won by 299 runs

Fifth Test: Melbourne, Jan 21–26
Australia 493–9 dec & 169–4 dec, England 392 & 161–0
Match drawn

Sixth Test: Adelaide, Jan 29–Feb 3
England 470 & 233–4 dec, Australia 235 & 328–3 dec
Match drawn

Seventh Test: Sydney, Feb 12–17
England 184 & 302, Australia 264 & 160
England won by 62 runs

Star performers

For Australia: Opener Keith Stackpole was in good nick, averaging 52.25.

For England: Opener Geoff Boycott, who topped the batting averages with 657 runs at an average of 93.85 and quickie John Snow, who took 31 wickets at 22.83 apiece.

They said it

"I've seen people hit by bottles and it makes a bloody mess of them." England captain **Ray Illingworth**, justifying his decision to lead his players off the field at Sydney

"In 1970/71 John Snow was at his peak, obtaining pace and movement off the seam and troubling all the upper order-batsmen." England batsman **Keith Fletcher**

— COUNTING DOWN TO VICTORY —

England's 2005 Ashes victory was sealed by a stubborn eighth-wicket stand at The Oval by centurion Kevin Pietersen and fifty-maker Ashley Giles. To the relief of a huge final-day crowd, the pair put on 109 runs to bat the Aussies out of the match and the series. But, as Giles later explained in a radio interview with Five Live, throughout their series-winning stand both batsmen were constantly aware that one mistake could see the end of England's Ashes dreams:

> "Basically, when I first went in, me and Kev were just trying to count down balls, then overs, then maybe 12 balls, and at one point we really pushed the boat out and got up to 30 balls to count down at a time. Every ball, Kev would come down the wicket and say 'Keep going, Gilo.' I did the same to him and we kept this going; slowly, slowly, we kept breaking these overs down, but it's amazing what you think the Australians can do when you're out there, how worried you are. We got to something where they would need 10 or 11 an over for 25 overs and we thought, 'We can't let them off the hook, surely they can't do this?' Realistically, they couldn't possibly – but you're always worried."

— ASHES PLAYERS LINKED WITH FEMALE CELEBRITIES —

Usman Afzaal (Eng): Amrita Arora (Bollywood actress)
Ian Botham (Eng): Lindy Field (former Miss Barbados)
Simon Jones (Eng): Jodie Kidd (model)
Kevin Pietersen (Eng): Vanessa Nimmo (Big Brother contestant), Caprice (model), Jessica Taylor (Liberty X singer)
Shane Warne (Aus): Liz Hurley (actress)

Talking of the fairer sex, England spinner Phil Tufnell certainly wasn't shy of fraternising with the locals on the Ashes tour of 1990/91. "There we all were, me and these four delicious darlings, all strawberry blonde with legs like stairways to heaven," he recalled in his autobiography. "I was like Billy Bunter with the keys to the tuck shop."

— MISTAKEN IDENTITY? —

Name	Ashes cricketer . . .	. . . or?
Michael Clarke	Australian batsman (2005–)	Drummer with 60s group The Byrds
Gary Gilmour	Australian all-rounder (1977)	Notorious US serial killer
David Lloyd	England opener (1974–75)	70s tennis player
Rodney Marsh	Australian wicketkeeper (1970–83)	England footballer of the 70s
Keith Miller	Australian all-rounder (1946–56)	*EastEnders* layabout
Charlie Parker	England spinner (1921)	US jazz maestro
Alan Smith	England wicketkeeper (1962–63)	Newcastle United striker
John Snow	England fast bowler (1968–75)	Nineteenth century doctor
Jack White	England spinner (1921)	White Stripes singer

— ASHES LEGENDS: GEOFF BOYCOTT —

One of his country's finest ever opening batsmen, Geoff Boycott's 18-year Test career included an England record 22 centuries.

Seven of those hundreds came against Australia, against whom Boycott made his Test debut in 1964, but one stands out above the others. At Boycott's home ground of Headingley in 1977, in front of an adoring public, he became the first player in history to reach 100 hundreds in a Test match. Typically, Boycott savoured the moment only briefly before regaining his composure, resuming his stance and continuing to go about his business of slowly and methodically accumulating runs. In the end, he only missed out on a double hundred by a mere handful of runs.

The fairytale was even more extraordinary than the bare facts suggest as Boycott had only just returned to the England team after a self-imposed absence of three years. Publicly, he stated that the reason for his period of exile was that he had lost his appetite for Test cricket, but the selectors' choice of Mike Denness as England's new captain in 1974 rather than Boycott himself was seen by many as the root cause of his dissatisfaction. Other critics suggested that Boycott simply wanted to avoid the world's best fast-bowling duo, the Australians Dennis Lillee and Jeff Thomson, while they were at their peaks.

That allegation was unfair as Boycott had a proven technique against pace bowling. Difficult to dislodge on even the most tricky of wickets, Boycott had a dour, dogged batting style which was nonetheless highly effective. Superb defensively, he rarely hit the ball in the air, favouring the on-drive and the square cut as his main run-scoring strokes. At Perth in 1978 he played an innings that summed up his no frills approach, making 77 runs without hitting a single boundary.

After marking his final Ashes appearance at The Oval in 1981 with a century, Boycott retired from international cricket after 108 Tests the following year. He went on to become a strident, controversial and opinionated commentator, overcoming a conviction in a French court for assault on a former lover in 1998 and a brush with cancer in 2003.

Geoff Boycott factfile
Born: Fitzwilliam, Yorkshire, 21 October 1940
County: Yorkshire
Ashes Tests: 38 (1964–81)
Batting: 2,945 (ave 47.50)
Bowling: 2 wickets (ave 58.50)

Others on Boycott

"His attention to the practical detail of equipment, and the minutiae of every stroke has probably never been rivalled."
Frank Tyson

"As I stood at the non-striker's end, I felt a wave of admiration for my partner; wiry, slight, dedicated, a lonely man doing a lonely job all these years."
Mike Brearley, during the 1978/79 Ashes tour

Geoff Boycott: The case for the defence

— RELUCTANT TO ECLIPSE THE DON —

In the Sydney Test of the 1946 Ashes series Syd Barnes and the great Don Bradman put on a mammoth 405 runs for the Aussies' fifth wicket, the second highest stand in the history of England-Australia clashes. Oddly, both men were out for the same score, 234, setting a record for the highest shared score by two batsmen in a first-class innings which still stands to this day.

In his autobiography, though, Barnes revealed that the statistical oddity was no mere coincidence, and that once Bradman was out he decided to give up his wicket without adding to his total. As he put it to an interviewer some years later: "It wouldn't be right for someone to make more runs than Sir Donald Bradman."

Presumably, he didn't feel quite the same way on those rare occasions when England bowled 'The Don' out cheaply!

— CLEM'S NERVOUS NINETIES —

Most batsmen get a little bit twitchy when they inch ever closer to a ton, especially in a contest with as much at stake as the Ashes. Happily, the majority manage to steer their way through the 'Nervous Nineties' and go on to experience the joyful relief of seeing three figures alongside their name on the scoreboard. Occasionally, though, nerves get the better of them and, rather than raising their bat in triumph, they end up trudging back to the pavilion just a handful of runs short of a century.

One player who became all too familiar with this particular form of disappointment was Australian legend Clem Hill, who was out a record five times in Ashes clashes while in the nineties. True, he did make four centuries against England in his long career (1896–1912), but that figure would have been significantly higher but for these missed opportunities, which included a hat-trick of dismissals for 99, 98 and 97 in three consecutive innings in 1902:

Year	Venue	Hill's Score	Dismissal method
1897	Sydney	96	Bowled
1902	Melbourne	99	Caught
1902	Adelaide	98	Caught
1902	Adelaide	97	Bowled
1912	Adelaide	98	Caught

— WHITEWASHED AGAIN! —

The 2006/07 Ashes series was one of the most keenly anticipated in history, but turned out to be a disappointingly one-sided affair as Australia hammered England 5–0 – the first 'whitewash' between the two sides since the Aussies won by the same convincing margin in 1920/21.

The tone of the series was set by the very first ball at Brisbane, when England's Steve Harmison sent his opening delivery careering off to second slip. Harmison had terrorised the Aussies during England's dramatic home victory in the 2005 series but the strike bowler's confidence appeared to be shattered after that first wayward ball. The Aussies took full advantage of England's bowling deficiencies to rattle up a first innings score in excess of 600 before dismissing their opponents for a paltry 157. After that, the outcome was never in doubt.

England put up a much better fight in the Second Test at Adelaide, and entertained hopes of levelling the series after a double century by Paul Collingwood and a scintillating 158 from Kevin Pietersen enabled them to declare at 551–6. Australia, though, hit back with a similar score thanks largely to centuries by captain Ricky Ponting and middle order batsman Michael Clarke. In their second innings England were dismissed for only 129, Shane Warne taking four wickets. Set just 168 to win, Australia reached their target fairly comfortably to win by six wickets.

The home side reclaimed the Ashes with a third consecutive victory in the next Test at Perth. After two low-scoring first innings, centuries by Michael Hussey, Michael Clarke and Adam Gilchrist put Australia in the driving seat and they went on to win by 206 runs, despite a battling second innings century by England opener Alistair Cook.

The visitors' confidence was now in shreds, and it was no surprise when they capitulated once more in the Fourth Test at Melbourne. As so often in the past, Aussie spin king Warne was their chief tormentor as Andrew Flintoff's men were bowled out for a totally inadequate 159 in the first innings. Centuries by Matthew Hayden and Andrew Symonds gave Australia a commanding lead and, following another poor batting display, England succumbed to an innings defeat.

In the final Test at Sydney the script was depressingly familiar. With Warne marking his last Test appearance before retirement with a swashbuckling 71, England were outclassed again and slumped to a ten-wicket defeat. Australia's victory rounded off an historic 5–0 drubbing which nobody, with the exception of ultra-confident Aussie pace bowler Glenn McGrath, had predicted after the closely fought series in England between the two sides just 18 months earlier.

— ALL OUT FOR 36 —

The lowest score in Ashes history is Australia's pitiful total of 36 at Edgbaston in 1902. Replying to England's total of 376–9 declared, the Aussies found themselves batting on a 'sticky wicket' following a thunderstorm. England left-arm spinner Wilfred Rhodes proved to be virtually unplayable, taking seven wickets for 17 runs as the Australian batsmen went down like skittles. Miraculously, however, the away side escaped with a draw when the heavens opened again and caused play to be abandoned.

England's lowest ever score against Australia is 45 all out at Sydney in 1887, Aussie seamers Charles Turner (6–15) and John Ferris (4–27) doing the damage while bowling unchanged from the start of the innings. Remarkably, England recovered from this setback to set the home side 111 to win in their second innings and, against the odds, dismissed the Australians for 97 to triumph by the narrow margin of 13 runs.

The two sides' lowest scores home and away are:

Team	Year	Venue	Score
Australia	1902	Edgbaston	36
Australia	1888	Sydney	42
England	1887	Sydney	45
England	1948	The Oval	52

— ASHES ODDITIES —

Some stranger than fiction stories from the 2005 series:

- At Old Trafford two fake umpires walked out of the pavilion at the start of play on the first day, just before the real ones emerged. The imposters were caught before entering the field of play, but reappeared at the Fourth Test at Trent Bridge where they reached the wicket before being apprehended. The pair were later both fined £70 under the Public Order Act.
- Retail sales fell 17% over the Saturday and Sunday of the thrilling Trent Bridge Test compared to the corresponding weekend in 2004. "It's pretty clear many people are watching the Ashes at the weekend rather than shopping," said the chief executive of Woolworths, Trevor Bish-Jones.
- A penthouse flat with a view of the Oval ground from the gas-holder side was let for the duration of the Test for £23,000.
- England's Ashes win sparked a row in the Scottish Parliament when Scottish Nationalist MSP Christine Grahame whinged about

excessive coverage being given to a sport of "only marginal interest in Scotland". A Conservative spokesperson hit back, claiming the Nationalists were being "petty and vindictive".

— ASHES LEGENDS: GREG CHAPPELL —

Hailing from a family steeped in Australian cricket, Greg Chappell was one of the greatest and most stylish batsmen of his generation.

Chappell's grandfather was Vic Richardson, a Test cricketer of the 1920s and 1930s, but an equally important influence was his older brother, Ian, who became Australian captain at the end of the 1970/71 series against England. Greg made his Test debut in the same series, notching an elegant century against Ray Illingworth's tourists at Perth. He continued to score heavily in Ashes clashes over the next dozen years, his total of nine centuries against England being bettered only by Don Bradman and Steve Waugh.

Chappell succeeded his brother as Australian captain in 1975, and went on to lead his country in 48 of the 87 Tests he appeared in, including the two Centenary Tests against England in 1977 and 1980. After briefly defecting to Kerry Packer's World Series, Chappell returned to the Australian side in the early '80s, resuming the captaincy for the victorious 1982/83 Ashes series. Less happily, Chappell was widely criticised when he instructed his younger brother, Trevor, to bowl the final ball of a One-Day international against New Zealand underarm, thus ensuring an Australian win.

After retiring as a player, Chappell became a respected cricket coach. In 2005, having previously worked for South Australia and the Pakistan National Cricket Academy, he was appointed coach of the Indian national team. He stayed in this post until 2007, resigning from the job after India's poor showing at the World Cup. Chappell's willingness to work for his country's opponents has not diminished his popularity at home, though, and in 2002 he was inducted into the Australian Cricket Hall of Fame.

Greg Chappell factfile
Born: Adelaide, 7 August 1948
State: South Australia, Queensland
County: Somerset
Ashes Tests: 35 (1970–83)
Batting: 2,619 runs (ave 45.94)
Bowling: 13 wickets (ave 52.33)

Others on Chappell

"It was as close to flawless as anything I have seen."
Richie Benaud on a Chappell century against England at Lord's in 1972

"Greg Chappell could not only tear an attack apart but he could also be so solid, so technically proficient. In form, he was a beautiful technician, as good as anyone."
Dennis Lillee

— ASHES RUNS: THE DON HEADS THE LIST —

No batsman has scored more runs in Ashes cricket than Aussie legend Don Bradman. 'The Don's' total of 5,028 runs puts him comfortably clear of his nearest rival, England's Jack Hobbs (3,636). Yet England's bowlers can consider that they got off relatively lightly against the Aussie run-machine as Bradman's average in Ashes matches (89.78) is fully ten runs lower than his overall Test average (99.94).

Otherwise, the list of top ten run-getters in England-Australia clashes is full of famous names, with English batsmen marginally having the edge:

Player	Tests	Innings	Not Out	Runs	HS	Ave
1. Don Bradman (Aus)	37	63	7	5,028	334	89.78
2. Jack Hobbs (Eng)	41	71	4	3,636	187	54.26
3. Allan Border (Aus)	47	82	19	3,548	200	56.31
4. David Gower (Eng)	42	77	4	3,269	215	44.78
5. Steve Waugh (Aus)	46	73	18	3,200	177*	58.18
6. Geoff Boycott (Eng)	38	71	9	2,945	191	47.50
7. Wally Hammond (Eng)	33	58	3	2,852	251	51.85
8. Herbert Sutcliffe (Eng)	27	46	5	2,741	194	66.85
9. Clem Hill (Aus)	41	76	1	2,660	188	35.46
10. John Edrich (Eng)	32	57	3	2,644	175	48.96

* not out

— ASHES VICTORY: CELEBRITY REACTION —

After England's dramatic victory in the 2005 Ashes series, celebrities from the worlds of sport, politics and showbusiness rushed to the nearest microphone to heap praise on Michael Vaughan's side. True, some of these celebs probably wouldn't know the difference between a cricket bat and a tennis racquet, but so what? If you were in the public eye, you simply had to have a view on the best piece of summer news since England won the 1966 World Cup.

Here's a small selection of post-victory quotes from some of the country's most famous names:

"My warmest congratulations to you, the England team and all the squad for the magnificent achievement of regaining the Ashes. This has been a truly memorable series and both sides can take credit for giving us all such a wonderfully exciting and entertaining summer of cricket at its best."

The Queen

"By bringing back the Ashes after so long you have given cricket a huge boost and lit up the whole summer."

Tony Blair, Labour Prime Minister

"It's a fantastic achievement. Congratulations to Michael Vaughan and the whole team. It has been a great series played in the best spirit and I wish I could have been there to witness it in person. We will be raising our glasses in New York."

Mick Jagger, Rolling Stones singer

"The whole country has been behind the team and I am sure it's been an inspiration to Michael Vaughan and his players. Everyone's fallen in love with cricket."

Steven Gerrard, Liverpool and England footballer

"I love watching England in whatever the sport is, but for the cricket team not only to win back the Ashes after such a long time, but also on home territory, was magnificent."

Kelly Holmes, 2004 Olympic Gold medal-winning athlete

— ASHES CRICKETERS TOP BBC POLL —

Just four England cricketers have been voted BBC Sports Personality of the Year since the award began in 1954, and each one of this quartet have collected the honour for their achievements in an Ashes series.

Spin bowler Jim Laker was the first cricketer to head the poll in 1956, thanks to his efforts in that year's tussle with the Aussies which included a world record 19 wickets in the Old Trafford Test.

Nineteen years later bespectacled middle-order batsman David Steele gained the viewers' votes for his brave defiance of Australian pace bowlers Dennis Lillee and Jeff Thomson. England lost that series in 1975 but six years later Ian Botham's heroics with bat and ball inspired his side to a famous Ashes victory. Come the end of the year and, to no one's surprise, 'Beefy' was a clear winner of the prestigious Beeb poll.

Making up the fab four is Andrew Flintoff, the acknowledged star of England's magnificent Ashes victory in 2005. Happily, 'Freddie's' team-mates were not forgotten by the voting public, who for the first time made England's cricketers the winners of the team award.

— HARMY'S NIGHTMARE FIRST BALL —

England's defence of the Ashes in the 2006/07 series Down Under got off to a bizarre start when the first ball of Steve Harmison's opening over veered wildly off the pitch towards second slip, where it was fielded by a surprised Andrew Flintoff. The (extremely) wide delivery got Australia off the mark in the First Test at Brisbane and, more significantly in the long term, dealt a crashing blow to Harmison's confidence.

"Anybody in my position having bowled a ball that wide would have had some mental flaw, some sort of psychological defect because of the nature of the game and what it stood for," the England paceman later admitted. "It was a long walk to the mark for the next ball and from there it didn't really get much better." Certainly, Harmison's series figures of just 10 wickets at a costly 61.40 runs each suggested he never quite recovered from that first ball disaster.

— ASHES LEGENDS: BOB WILLIS —

Only Ian Botham has taken more wickets in Ashes Tests for England than Bob Willis, a lanky fast bowler with a shock of frizzy brown-red hair and a famously long run up.

Willis, like Botham, enjoyed his finest hour in an England shirt against the Aussies at Headingley in 1981. After Botham's blistering batting performance had given the home side an outside chance of victory, a magnificent spell of all-out fast bowling by Willis saw the Aussies crumble to an unlikely defeat. The eight wickets Willis collected in the innings not only turned the match, but also an Ashes series that looked to be heading Australia's way. Yet, remarkably, Willis very nearly missed his day of glory having originally been left out of the side due to a chest infection. "I effectively talked my way back into the team," he recalled later of a long discussion with the England selectors in which he persuaded them of his fitness.

It was hardly unusual for there to be question marks over Willis's physical condition. After making his debut as a replacement for the injured Alan Ward on the 1970/71 Ashes tour, the injury-prone Willis struggled to establish himself in the England side, only really emerging as a regular in the late seventies under the leadership of Mike Brearley. Nonetheless, he went on to play in 90 Tests, captaining the side in 18 matches, including the unsuccessful 1982/83 tour of Australia.

A huge fan of the singer Bob Dylan, Willis changed his name by deed poll to 'Robert George Dylan Willis'. He is now a pundit on Sky TV but, in much the same way that Dylan's whining vocals are not to everyone's taste, Willis's somewhat lugubrious delivery behind the mic has divided opinion among viewers.

Bob Willis factfile
Born: Sunderland, 30 May 1949
County: Surrey, Warwickshire
Ashes Tests: 35 (1971–83)
Batting: 382 runs (ave 10.32)
Bowling: 128 wickets (ave 26.14)

Others on Willis

"A 1914 biplane tied up with elastic bands trying vainly to take off."
Guardian writer **Frank Keating** on Willis's run up

"It was the greatest one-off sustained effort I ever saw from a fast bowler in the entire time I played cricket."
Dennis Lillee on Willis's eight-wicket haul at Headingley in 1981

—HAT-TRICKS —

Australian quick Peter Siddle celebrated his 26th birthday in fine style on the first day of the First Test at Brisbane in 2010 by taking a hat-trick – only the third bowler to pull off this feat in modern Ashes history. England opener Alastair Cook was the first to fall to the Aussie paceman, edging to slip where Shane Watson snaffled the catch. Siddle then bowled Matt Prior through the gate for a golden duck, before taking a third wicket in three balls by firing a yorker into the pads of Stuart Broad.

Apart from Siddle, Australia's Shane Warne and England's Darren Gough are the only other bowlers to claim hat-tricks in recent Ashes encounters. The Aussie spin supremo was the first to strike, taking three English wickets in consecutive balls in the 1994 Melbourne Test. Warne's first victim was Phil DeFreitas, who was given out lbw. Next up, ironically, was Darren Gough who fell to a catch behind the stumps by Ian Healy. No doubt to Warne's delight, the next Englishman in was fast bowler Devon Malcolm, a renowned 'rabbit' with the bat. Surrounded by Aussie fielders, Malcolm prodded at Warne's delivery and only succeeded in spooning an easy catch to David Boon. The hat-trick was in the bag, and the only surprise was that Warne didn't claim a fourth straight wicket as England's last man in was Phil 'The Cat' Tufnell – an even worse batsman than Malcolm!

Warne's hat-trick was the first in Ashes cricket since 1904, when Australia's Hugh Trumble pulled off an identical feat at Melbourne. Trumble had previously recorded another hat-trick in the 1901/02 series, yet again at Melbourne, to make him the only bowler in Ashes history to have two hat-tricks to his name.

Five years after Warne's historic feat, Darren Gough matched the Aussie legend by taking a hat-trick of his own in the Sydney Test of 1999. Dazzer's victims in Australia's first innings were Ian Healy, caught behind by wicketkeeper Warren Hegg, and Stuart MacGill and Colin Miller, both of whom were clean bowled by the Yorkshire paceman. In all, there have been nine hat-tricks in Ashes history:

Bowler	Year	Venue	Batsmen dismissed
Fred Spofforth (Aus)	1879	Melbourne	Royle, MacKinnon, Emmett
Billy Bates (Eng)	1883	Melbourne	McDonnell, G Giffen, Bonner
Johnny Briggs (Eng)	1892	Sydney	W Giffen, Callaway, Blackham
Jack Hearne (Eng)	1899	Leeds	Hill, Gregory, Noble
Hugh Trumble (Aus)	1902	Melbourne	Jones, Gunn, Barnes

Hugh Trumble (Aus)	1904	Melbourne	Bosanquet, Warner, Lilley
Shane Warne (Aus)	1994	Melbourne	DeFreitas, Gough, Malcolm
Darren Gough (Eng)	1999	Sydney	Healy, MacGill, Miller
Peter Siddle (Aus)	2010	Brisbane	Cook, Prior, Broad

— STEVE'S TON IS TOP ASHES MOMENT FOR AUSSIES —

In late 2005 listeners to Australian radio station ABC were asked to vote for the most memorable sporting moments in their country's history. Three Ashes moments made it into the top 25, with Steve Waugh's 'Perfect Day' century against England in 2003 obtaining the highest placing at number five. Shane Warne's spectacular dismissal of Mike Gatting with his first delivery in Ashes cricket came in at number eight, while the whole of the 2005 series between England and Australia was listed at number 18 in the poll. Somehow, we suspect it might have finished higher if the Aussies had won the series!

Strangely, from an English perspective at least, the poll was topped by some super-rich men messing about in a boat (Australia II's success in the 1983 America's Cup), while the Socceroos' qualification for the 2006 World Cup came in second. That, by the way, is the very same World Cup that England *won* in 1966!

— NO JOY FOR BOWLERS —

On just two days in Ashes cricket the bowlers have toiled through three full sessions for absolutely no reward. On the third day of the Melbourne Test in 1925, England openers Jack Hobbs and Herbert Sutcliffe occupied the crease from first ball to last, while scoring 283–0. Incredibly, Australia still managed to win this timeless Test by 81 runs on the seventh day of play.

Sadly for England, history did not repeat itself after Aussie openers Geoff Marsh and Mark Taylor scored 310–0 on the first day of the Trent Bridge Test in 1989. The massive opening stand provided the platform for the tourists' crushing victory by an innings and 180 runs.

— MEN OF THE MATCH 2006/07 —

Test	Venue	Man of the Match
First	Brisbane	Ricky Ponting (Australia)
Second	Adelaide	Ricky Ponting (Australia)
Third	Perth	Michael Hussey (Australia)
Fourth	Melbourne	Shane Warne (Australia)
Fifth	Sydney	Stuart Clark (Australia)

In addition to these awards, Aussie captain Ricky Ponting was also named as Man of the Series.

— YOUNGEST AND OLDEST CENTURIONS —

The youngest batsman to score a century in Ashes cricket is Australia's Archie Jackson. The stroke-playing opener was just 19 and 152 days when he notched 164 at Adelaide on his Test debut in 1929. Tragically, Jackson was never to fulfill his huge potential as he died a few years later from tuberculosis, aged just 23.

Legendary middle order batsman Denis Compton holds the same record for England, scoring 102 at Trent Bridge in 1938 aged 20 and 19 days.

At the other end of the age scale, Jacks Hobbs was 82 days past his 46th birthday when he struck the last of his 12 Ashes centuries, notching 142 at Melbourne in 1929.

— THE GREAT ASHES SERIES: 'LILLEE AND THOMMO ON THE ATTACK', AUSTRALIA 1974/75 —

The abiding image of this series Down Under was of nervous-looking English batsmen dodging and weaving to avoid a barrage of bouncers sent down by a pair of aggressive Aussie quicks, established star Dennis Lillee and newcomer Jeff Thomson. Occasionally, ball would strike flesh and, to roars of delight from the packed stands, an English batsman would crumple up in pain or tentatively pull off a glove to rub his bruised knuckles.

In many ways, this was the Australians' revenge for Bodyline, some 40 years on – and, like that famous encounter, there was only ever going to be one winner. The tone for the series was set in the First Test at Brisbane when Lillee and Thomson took 13 of the English wickets as Australia won by a comfortable margin.

Two English batsmen, John Edrich and Dennis Amiss, suffered hand fractures during the match so the veteran Colin Cowdrey was hurriedly flown over to Australia as cover. He scored a battling 41 in England's second innings in the Second Test in Perth, but it was nowhere near enough to prevent the tourists going down to another heavy defeat.

England put up a better fight in the Third Test in Melbourne, an even match ending in a draw after the Aussies finished eight runs short of victory with two wickets remaining. Despite this improved showing, out-of-form England skipper Mike Denness took the drastic measure of dropping himself for the Fourth Test in Sydney. John Edrich replaced Denness as captain but it made no difference, as the Aussies dominated proceedings again. Ian Redpath and Ian Chappell both hit centuries to leave England needing 390 to win in their second innings and, predictably, they fell well short, with Aussie spinner Ashley Mallett (4–21) doing much of the damage.

That victory guaranteed that Australia would reclaim the Ashes, but the home side were in no mood to let up in the Fifth Test in Adelaide. Although Jeff Thomson was unable to bowl in England's second innings after picking up an injury playing tennis on the rest day, the visiting batsmen, with the honourable exception of centurion Alan Knott, were as ineffectual as they had been all series. Yet again, the Aussies won by a distance.

The series-long script only changed in the final Test in Melbourne when England's batsman, especially century makers Mike Denness and Keith Fletcher, took advantage of Thomson's absence and an injury to Dennis Lillee to win by an innings. For England's battered and bruised touring party the victory was some consolation, but no one was under any illusion that it was far too little, far too late.

First Test: Brisbane, Nov 29–Dec 4
Australia 309 & 288–5 dec, England 265 & 166
Australia won by 166 runs

Second Test: Perth, Dec 13–17
England 208 & 293, Australia 481 & 23–1
Australia won by nine wickets

Third Test: Melbourne, Dec 26–31
England 242 & 244, Australia 241 & 238–8
Match drawn

Fourth Test: Sydney, Jan 4–9
Australia 405 & 289–4 dec, England 295 & 228
Australia won by 171 runs

Fifth Test: Adelaide, Jan 25–30
Australia 304 & 272–5 dec, England 172 & 241
Australia won by 163 runs

Sixth Test: Melbourne, Feb 8–13
Australia 152 & 373, England 529
England won by an innings and 4 runs

Star performers

For Australia: Fast bowling duo Dennis Lillee (25 wickets) and Jeff Thomson (33 wickets) were too hot to handle for the English batsmen.

For England: Tony Greig (average 41.7) was the pick of England's under-achieving batsmen and also pitched in with 17 wickets.

They said it
"England were not very happy with the aggressive way in which we approached the game and not many of them stayed around for a drink after play."
Dennis Lillee

"The sound of the ball hitting the batsman's skull was music to my ears."
Jeff Thomson

— INDIAN SIGN —

Somewhat bizarrely, the first four players of Indian extraction to appear for England against Australia all notched centuries on their Ashes debuts. The high-scoring quartet were:

- **KS Ranjitsinhji:** An Indian prince, the glamorous Ranjitsinjhi hit a swashbuckling 154 not out in the second innings of the 1896 Old Trafford Test. He later represented India at the League of Nations.
- **KS Duleepsinhji:** The nephew of Ranjitsinjhi, 'Duleep' scored 173 against the Aussies at Lord's in 1930. When he played a rash stroke and was caught in the outfield his uncle reportedly remarked, "He was always a careless lad."
- **Nawab of Pataudi:** The Nawab scored 102 in the First Test at Sydney in 1932 but, after making clear his opposition to England captain Douglas Jardine's Bodyline tactics, returned home from the tour shortly before the Third Test. He later died, aged just 42, while playing polo.
- **Subba Row:** Born in London of Indian parents, Subba Row marked his Ashes debut by hitting 112 at Edgbaston in 1961. He also made a century in the Oval Test, but at the end of the series abruptly retired from cricket to pursue his business interests. He later became chairman of the Test and County Cricket Board.

— DOUGLAS JARDINE: HERO OR VILLAIN? —

England captain from 1931 to 1934, Douglas Jardine was largely responsible for the controversy that raged in Australia during the infamous Bodyline series in 1932/33.

Born in India in 1900 of Scottish descent, Jardine attended Oxford University before winning his first England call up as a Surrey player in 1928. Later that same year he went on the successful MCC tour of Australia, where he developed an intense dislike of both the country and its people. Jeered by the home crowd for his somewhat haughty attitude and preference for an Oxford University Harlequin cap, Jardine responded by telling one Australian player, "All Australians are uneducated and an unruly mob."

Business engagements prevented Jardine from playing in the 1930 Ashes series in England, but he keenly followed the exploits of Australia's star batsman Don Bradman, who averaged a phenomenal 139.14 in the five Tests.

Appointed England captain for the 1932/33 tour of Australia, Jardine knew that he had to devise a plan to counter Bradman's run-scoring ability. After speaking to the Nottinghamshire and England fast bowlers Harold Larwood and Bill Voce, the new England skipper decided that Bradman, although clearly a great batsman, had a weakness against short-pitched bowling. Jardine believed that Bradman – or 'the little bastard', as he preferred to call him – would be unsettled by a barrage of deliveries aimed at the body rather than the wicket, especially if a phalanx of alert fielders were placed on the leg side waiting for a possible catch.

Bodyline, or 'leg theory' as Jardine called it, proved a hugely effective tactic in the series, which England won 4–1. The Australians, however, were outraged by a strategy which they believed was both dangerous and unsportsmanlike. After two Australian batsmen, including the captain Bill Woodfull, were injured after being hit by short-pitched deliveries in the Third Test at Adelaide, the Australian Board of Control sent an angry fax condemning Bodyline to the MCC. For a while, the rest of the tour was in doubt and relations between the two countries were strained to breaking point.

Jardine, though, remained unrepentant about his role in the controversy. Nevertheless, he wasn't quite the ogre he was depicted as being in the Australian press. After Aussie wicketkeeper Bert Oldfield was struck on the head at Adelaide and rushed to hospital, for instance, Jardine sent a telegram of sympathy to Oldfield's wife and arranged for presents to be given to the couple's daughters. Sadly, he never had the opportunity of mending fences with his old adversaries as he turned down the chance to captain England in the 1934 Ashes series and soon retired from first-class cricket to become a journalist.

Even today, the mere mention of Jardine's name can stir strong emotions in patriotic Australians. For example, commentator Alan McGilvray once described him as "The most notorious Englishman since Jack The Ripper." Among his players, though, Jardine was respected as a superb leader and a fine batsman. "To me and every member of the 1932/33 MCC side in Australia, Douglas Jardine was the greatest captain England ever had," said former England bowler Bill Bowes at the time of Jardine's death from lung cancer in 1958. "He was a great fighter, a good friend and an unforgiving enemy."

The controversial Douglas Jardine

— WARNE'S LANDMARKS —

The first bowler to take 700 Test wickets, Shane Warne reached the following important milestones in Ashes matches:

Wicket	Year	Venue	Batsman	How out
50th	1993	Trent Bridge	Nasser Hussain	c Boon b Warne
250th	1997	Old Trafford	Alec Stewart	b Warne
400th	2001	The Oval	Alec Stewart	c Gilchrist b Warne
600th	2005	Old Trafford	Marcus Trescothick	c Gilchrist b Warne
700th	2006	Melbourne	Andrew Strauss	b Warne

— DOUBLE-WINNING ENGLAND SKIPPERS —

Only three England captains have led their country to victory both home and away in full Ashes series consisting of a minimum of five Tests:

Captain	Home series wins	Away series wins
Sir Len Hutton	1953	1954/55
Mike Brearley	1977, 1981*	1978/79
Andrew Strauss	2009	2010/11

* Replaced Ian Botham as captain after the Second Test

— UNLIKELY TOP SCORER —

On just one occasion in Ashes history has the number 11 shown up the rest of his team-mates by making the biggest single score in an innings. That was way back in 1885 when legendary Australian fast bowler Fred 'The Demon' Spofforth top scored with a battling 50 in his side's total of 163 in the Fifth Test at Melbourne. However, his batting heroics were not sufficient to prevent his team from going down to defeat by an innings and 98 runs – a result which clinched a 3–2 series win for the English tourists led by skipper Arthur Shrewsbury.

— THREE PAIRS —

The only instance of three different batsmen picking up pairs in the same Ashes Test occurred at Adelaide in 1975. England's Dennis Amiss, Geoff Arnold and Derek Underwood all failed to bother the scorer in either innings. Unsurprisingly, given this minimal contribution from three of their players, the tourists went down to a heavy defeat losing by 163 runs.

— EXPENSIVE WICKET —

The following players had the satisfaction of taking a single wicket in Ashes matches, but it cost them – the opposition taking more than 100 runs off their bowling overall:

Year	Bowler	Venue dismissed conceded	Batsman runs	Total
1885	Jack Worrall (Aus)	Melbourne	William Attewell	127
1894	Francis Ford (Eng)	Sydney	Frank Iredale	129
1920	Abe Waddington (Eng)	Sydney	Charles Macartney	119
1921	Tommy Andrews (Aus)	Old Trafford	Ciss Parkin	116
1925	Albert Hartkopf (Aus)	Melbourne	Bert Strudwick	134
1933	Harry Alexander (Aus)	Sydney	Hedley Verity	154
1938	Mervyn Waite (Aus)	The Oval	Denis Compton	190
1951	John Warr (Eng)	Adelaide	Ian Johnson	281

Perhaps the most unlikely of these wickets was the one taken by Australian all-rounder Mervyn Waite, who bowled Denis Compton for just a single run during England's world record innings of 903–7 declared at The Oval in 1938. Waite certainly savoured the moment, as Compton later recalled: "This was the only wicket he took in his Test career and he became so proud of his achievement that every time I arrived in Australia or he in England, he would ring to arrange to buy me a 'thank you' drink."

— ASHES LEGENDS: DENNIS LILLEE —

Dennis Lillee was one of the main reasons why English batsmen spent much of the 1970s nervously ducking for cover – and, occasionally, checking they still had all their teeth. A fast bowler who also counted variations in pace, length and movement in his armoury, Lillee always seemed to reserve his best for Ashes clashes. Indeed, no fewer than 167 of his 355 Test wickets were taken against England – an Ashes record that was only surpassed by Shane Warne in 2005.

Lillee made his Test debut against England at Adelaide in 1971, but it was on the following year's Ashes tour that he really made his mark in international cricket, taking 31 wickets at an impressive average of 17.67.

Recovered from a back injury that threatened his career, Lillee then formed a frighteningly fast partnership with fellow quick Jeff Thomson for the successful 1974/75 Ashes series. The pair were simply too quick and aggressive for the English batsmen, some of whom were clearly rattled by the artillery barrage the duo unleashed. A fiery character with a bristling moustache, Lillee revelled in his opponents' discomfort, saying "I try to hit a batsman in the ribcage when I bowl a purposeful bouncer, and I want it to hurt so much that the batsman doesn't want to face me any more."

In 1977 Lillee joined Kerry Packer's World Series Cricket but he later returned to the Test arena. While not as quick as in his heyday, he still exhibited the copybook action and metronomic accuracy that were two of his trademarks. Lillee eventually retired from Test cricket in 1984, but carried on playing for Tasmania in the Sheffield Shield until 1988.

Since he packed up playing, Lillee has become a renowned fast bowling coach. As player and coach Lillee's contribution to Australian cricket has been enormous, and was officially recognised in 2002 when he was inducted into his country's Cricket Hall of Fame. A cult hero to antipodean sports fans, Lillee's fans include Aussie band Men at Work who famously namechecked him in their song *No Restrictions* ("Hear the cricket calling, switch on the TV, and sit and stare for hours, cheering Dennis Lillee").

Dennis Lillee factfile
Born: Subiaco, Western Australia, 18 July 1949
State: Western Australia, Tasmania
County: Northants
Ashes Tests: 29 (1971–82)
Batting: 469 runs (ave 18.04)
Bowling: 167 wickets (ave 21.00)

Others on Lillee

"Lillee will always be a better bowler than me."
Ian Botham, after breaking Lillee's Test wicket-taking record

"He had everything: courage, variety, high morale, arrogance, supreme fitness and aggression."
Former England captain **Bob Willis**

Dennis Lillee took 167 English wickets

— RADIO FIVE LIVE SPORTING CENTURY POLL —

In 2003 radio station Five Live asked listeners to vote for their favourite sporting moments. The poll, which was headed by England's 1966 World Cup triumph, featured the following Ashes moments in the top hundred:

2. Ian Botham's century at Headingley, 1981
52. The Bodyline tour, 1932/33
74. Jim Laker takes all ten Australian wickets at Old Trafford, 1956
92. Denis Compton hits the winning runs for England to reclaim the Ashes, 1953
99. Len Hutton's record 364 at The Oval, 1938

— TWO-TON SUTCLIFFE STILL A LOSER —

In the Second Test at Melbourne in 1925 England opener Herbert Sutcliffe became the first batsman in Test history to score a century in both innings yet still end up on the losing side. Replying to Australia's total of 600, Sutcliffe (176) and Jack Hobbs (154) both made tons in an opening stand of 283 before England collapsed to 479 all out. After Australia were dismissed for 250 in their second innings, England had an outside chance of victory but despite another valiant effort from Sutcliffe, who made 127, they were bowled out for 290 to lose by 81 runs.

— THE GREAT ASHES SERIES: BOTHAM'S ASHES, ENGLAND 1981 —

The 1981 series will forever be associated with the heroics of Ian Botham, who at times appeared to be playing the Australians on his own. What is less often remembered, though, is that the summer began miserably for Both, who felt compelled to resign as England captain after bagging a pair in the drawn Second Test at Lord's.

By that time, Australia were already leading 1–0, having won a low-scoring match at Trent Bridge by four wickets, Terry Alderman taking nine wickets on his Test debut for the Aussies.

Following his personal nightmare at Lord's, Botham was replaced as England captain by Mike Brearley, an opening batsman with a relatively poor record in Test cricket but a master tactician and an astute man-manager. Part of Brearley's brief was to get the best out of the underperforming Botham, and he certainly did that at Headingley. However, for most of the match it appeared that England would go down to a heavy defeat.

Following on, the home side were in dire trouble until a whirlwind century by Botham at least gave them something to bowl at. Nevertheless, the Australian target was only a measly 129 runs and, after a steady start, the visitors seemed to be cruising to a straightforward win. England fast bowler Bob Willis, though, had other ideas and in a fiery spell of 8–43 took the wickets which gave Brearley's men the most unlikely of victories.

There was a similar denouement in the Fourth Test at Edgbaston, where Australia only needed 151 to win a low-scoring match. With 45 required and five wickets remaining Kim Hughes' side appeared to be firm favourites – until Botham came on to bowl and promptly took all five Aussie wickets for just one run. For the second time in a month, the England players ran from the pitch triumphantly brandishing the stumps while the Aussies slunk away in disbelief.

Botham was again the star of the Old Trafford Test, hitting a six-filled century off just 86 balls to set Australia a mountainous target. Despite centuries from Allan Border and Graham Yallop they fell 103 runs short and England retained the Ashes.

The final Test at The Oval was an entertaining draw, notable for a last Ashes century by England opener Geoff Boycott and a debut ton for Aussie middle-order batsman Dirk Welham. Oh, and Ian Botham took ten wickets in the match – in a summer when Both was never out of the news, it was almost inevitable that England's superstar all-rounder would have the last word.

First Test: Trent Bridge, June 18–21
England 185 & 125, Australia 179 & 132–6
Australia won by four wickets

Second Test: Lord's, July 2–7
England 311 & 265–8 dec, Australia 345 & 90–4
Match drawn

Third Test: Headingley, July 16–21
Australia 401–9 dec & 111, England 174 & 356
England won by 18 runs

Fourth Test: Edgbaston, July 30–Aug 2
England 189 & 219, Australia 258 & 121
England won by 29 runs
Botham five wickets for one run in 28 balls

Fifth Test: Old Trafford, Aug 13–17
England 231 & 404, Australia 130 & 402
England won by 103 runs
Botham 118 off 102 balls

Sixth Test: The Oval, Aug 27–Sept 1
Australia 352 & 344–9 dec, England 314 & 261–7 dec
Match drawn

Star performers

For England: No contest – from the Third Test onwards Ian Botham dominated the series with bat and ball.

For Australia: With an Australian Ashes record of 42 wickets, Terry Alderman didn't deserve to be on the losing side.

They said it

"It was just one of those crazy, glorious, one-off flukes."
Ian Botham, on England's unexpected victory at Headingley

"This series will be remembered in 100 years – unfortunately."
Kim Hughes, Australia captain

— THE CURSE OF NELSON AND THE DEVIL'S NUMBER —

Every England batsman knows that soon after passing the century mark he will face another tricky challenge – namely, negotiating his way past 111, a number associated with bad luck as it is supposed to represent the eye, arm and leg lost by Admiral Nelson (let's forget for a moment that Nelson didn't lose a leg, it's the myth that's important here!).

However, in Ashes battles at least, 'Nelson' has not proved a particularly unlucky number. Indeed, just two England batsman have been dismissed for 111 against Australia – Bill Edrich at Headingley in 1948 and Tom Graveney at Sydney in 1955. In addition to this pair, Maurice Leyland made 111 not out at Melbourne in 1937.

Superstitious Aussies, meanwhile, tend to get twitchy when they reach 87 – the so-called 'Devil's Number' is said to be unlucky because it is 13 short of a hundred. Again, though, there is little evidence to suggest that an Australian batsman on 87 is especially likely to lose his wicket. In fact, the history books show that just five Aussies have been dismissed for this score against England, with Keith Stackpole being the most recent at Adelaide way back in 1971.

— CHUCK TOILS FOR LITTLE REWARD —

At the famous 1938 Test at The Oval when England scored a world record 903–7 declared, all the Aussie bowlers suffered some severe punishment at the hands of Hutton and co. but none more so than Leslie 'Chuck' Fleetwood-Smith. Over the course of 85 overs the leg-break and googly bowler conceded an incredible 298 runs, a world record for Test cricket which still stands today. True, Fleetwood-Smith did manage to capture the prize wicket of Wally Hammond, but the pounding he took in south London in his last ever Test match had a dramatic effect on his bowling average, knocking it down from 31.02 before the game to a distinctly less impressive 37.38 afterwards.

— BENDING THE RULES —

There's no love lost between England and Australia at the best of times. Little wonder, then, that Ashes clashes down the years have been full of incidents where one side or the other has accused the opposition of gamesmanship or, even, downright cheating:

- In the famous 1882 Oval Test which gave birth to the Ashes legend, a decent second innings partnership was developing between Australian captain Billy Murdoch and Sammy Jones. After running a single, Jones left his crease to pat down the pitch. While Jones was doing his 'gardening', England fielder WG Grace cheekily whipped off the bails and successfully appealed for a run-out. The Aussies were furious and fired off a barrage of insults in Grace's direction, but they had the last laugh when they won the match by just seven runs.
- Bodyline, 1932. The England bowlers' practice of targeting the Australian batsmen rather than the wicket was condemned by all and sundry Down Under, from the Aussie captain Bill Woodfull to the Australian Cricket Board, which sent an irate telegram to MCC headquarters at Lord's.
- In the famous Old Trafford Test of 1956 when Jim Laker took 19 wickets in the match, Australian captain Ian Johnson tried to get play suspended when the sawdust on the damp pitch blew into his eyes while he batted.
- England accused no fewer than four Australian bowlers of being 'chuckers' on their tour Down Under in 1958/59. The bowling actions of seamers Ian Meckiff, Keith Slater and Gordon Rorke and spinner Jim Burke were all under the microscope while there were suspicions too that Rorke was often well past the bowling crease when he let

his delivery go due to a lengthy drag. "It was like standing in the middle of a darts match," joked England's Jim Laker. No measures were taken against any of the bowlers during the series, but Meckiff's cricket career came to a grinding halt when he was called four times for throwing in a Test against South Africa in 1963.

- Trent Bridge, 2005. After being run out by England substitute fielder Gary Pratt, Aussie captain Ricky Ponting launched into a vitriolic tirade against Michael Vaughan's use of subs. "I think it is an absolute disgrace the spirit of the game is being treated like that," fumed Ponting. "Duncan Fletcher has known right through the summer this is something we haven't been happy with, but it's continued. He knows it's something that has got under our skins and I've had enough of it, and I let him know that, and most of his players too." Ponting's rant earned him a hefty fine and, among English fans at least, a reputation as a bad loser.

- Australia captain Ricky Ponting was left fuming again in 2009 when England's delaying tactics in the First Test at Sophia Gardens, Cardiff, helped the home side cling on for an unlikely draw. Down to their last-wicket pair of Jimmy Anderson and Monty Panesar, England were understandably keen to prevent the Aussies from racing through the overs as the clock ticked on to close of play, and managed to waste a few minutes by sending out twelfth man Bilal Shafayat to offer the batsmen new gloves and physio Steve McCoy to check on the players' physical condition. Needless to say, Ponting was distinctly unimpressed. "I didn't see anyone call for the pyhsio to come out," he whinged afterwards. "As far as I'm concerned, it was pretty ordinary, really. But they can play whatever way they want to play."

— THEY SAID IT 2 —

"Are you aware, sir, that the last time I saw anything like that on a top lip, the whole head had to be destroyed?"
Comedian **Eric Morecame** to Dennis Lillee, who sported a thick black moustache throughout his long playing career

"The Aussies try to present a tough-guy image, but this present generation are a bunch of sissies."
Tony Greig, 1996

"Playing against a team with Ian Chappell as captain turns a cricket match into gang warfare."
England captain **Mike Brearley**

"The aim of English Test cricket is, in fact, mainly to beat Australia."
Jim Laker

"I enjoy hitting a batsman more than getting him out. I like to see blood on the pitch."
Jeff Thomson

"I don't mind seeing blood on the pitch."
Jason Gillespie

"Test cricket is not a light-hearted business, especially that between England and Australia."
Donald Bradman

"Cricket needs brightening up a bit. My solution is to let the players drink at the beginning of the game, not after. It always works in our picnic matches."
Paul Hogan, Australian comedian and actor

"McCague will go down in Test cricket history as the rat who joined the sinking ship."
Daily Telegraph Mirror in Sydney on **Martin McCague's** 1993 selection by England against Australia, the country where he had been raised

"England have only three major problems. They can't bat, they can't bowl and they can't field."
Cricket writer **Martin Johnson's** assessment in *The Independent* of England's 1986/87 touring party of Australia. They returned having retained the Ashes, leading Johnson to say, 'Right quote, wrong team'

"Chappell was a coward. He needed a crowd around him before he would say anything. He was sour like milk that had been sitting in the sun for a week."
Ian Botham on Australia captain Ian Chappell

"The main thing about him is that he is so mentally tough that he thrives on big-match situations."
Geoffrey Boycott on Kevin Pietersen, September 2005

"If you're playing against the Australians, you don't walk."
Ian Botham, 1996

— A SIX-PACK OF SMITHS —

Unsurprisingly, more cricketers called Smith have represented England in Ashes cricket than players with any other surname. To date, six Smiths have pulled on the Three Lions sweater against the Aussies and they are:

- **Ernest 'Tiger' Smith (1911–12):** Wicketkeeper whose poor batting technique prevented him from winning more Test caps. He later became an umpire.
- **Smith (1946–47):** Leg break and googly bowler who originally thought he'd been called up for Test match action in 1933. Sadly, the telegram Smith had been sent informing him of his selection turned out to be a hoax. He eventually made his Test bow against Australia in 1946.
- **MJK Smith (1961–72):** Bespectacled right-hand batsmen who captained England in half of his 50 Tests but, nonetheless, was never sure of his place. Also played in a rugby international for England against Wales in 1956.
- **Smith (1962–63):** Wicketkeeper who played in four Tests in the drawn Ashes series in Australia in 1962/63 but, the following season, lost his place to Jim Parks.
- **Smith (1989–93):** South African-born batsmen who made his best Ashes score, 143, at Old Trafford in 1989. His older brother, Chris, also played Test cricket for England but never lined up against the Aussies.
- **Smith (1997):** Swing bowler whose less than impressive display against the Aussies at Headingley in 1997 ensured he was never called up by England again.

— TEST WASH-OUT LEADS TO ONE-DAY HISTORY —

The 1970/71 Melbourne Test was the third in Ashes history to be abandoned without a ball being bowled, after similar wash-outs in 1890 and 1938. However, the organisers were determined not to let the bad weather ruin everybody's fun and, on what should have been the final day of the Test, Australia and England faced each other in the world's first ever one-day international.

The 40 eight-ball over a-side match attracted a crowd of 46,006 to the MCG, and the fans who turned up were rewarded with a reasonably exciting game. Batting first, England were all out for 190 in 39.4 overs, John Edrich making 82. In reply, Australia reached 191–5 in 34.6 overs to win by five wickets.

The experiment had been a success, and one-day matches were very soon an established part of the international cricket scene.

— ASHES LEGENDS: ALLAN BORDER —

Australia captain in a record 29 Ashes Tests, the second top Aussie run-getter against England behind Sir Donald Bradman and the first batsman to score more than 11,000 runs in Test cricket – these are just some of Allan Border's achievements in a 16-year international career which began with his debut against England in 1978.

A gutsy, pugnacious left-handed batsman, Border was no stylist but he was one of cricket's most successful accumulators of runs. Strong off his legs and a fine driver through midwicket, he was also a patient builder of an innings – in contrast to some of his flashier contemporaries. As Australian skipper from 1985 to 1994 he was an effective leader, although his spiky dealings with the British press led to him being dubbed 'Captain Grumpy'.

Having been on the losing side in his first two Ashes series as Aussie captain, Border finally led his team to victory in 1989. The Aussies' 4–0 win marked a turning point in the fortunes of the two countries, and began an era of Australian domination which would not end until 2005. After retaining the Ashes in 1990/91 with a 3–0 home victory, Border's men recorded another convincing win, 4–1, in England in 1993. Although nearing the end of his career, Border still managed to post his highest ever score against England in this series, 200 not out at Headingley.

After a then record 156 Tests, Border retired in 1994. Four years later he became an Australian selector, a position he held until 2005 when he stood down to concentrate on his media career. Border was inducted into the Australian Cricket Hall of Fame in 2000 and, in a further mark of the esteem in which he is held Down Under, from 2000 the Australian Player of the Year has been presented with the Allan Border Medal.

Allan Border factfile
Born: Sydney, 27 July 1955
State: New South Wales, Queensland
County: Essex, Gloucestershire
Ashes Tests: 47 (1978–93)
Batting: 3,548 runs (ave 56.31)
Bowling: 4 wickets (ave 93.50)

Others on Border

"You had to respect him for his gutsy attitude. He was a dogged player who could also play some very good shots, bowl a bit and was a top fielder. In other words, he was a very good cricketer and a good team person."
Dennis Lillee

"Border has not so much a style as a *modus operandi*. He is utterly practical."
John Woodcock in *The Times*

— BEYOND THE CALL OF DUTY —

Ashes players who carried on batting when lesser mortals might have opted for the 'retired hurt' option:

- **Warwick Armstrong (Aus), Melbourne, 1921:** Nicknamed 'The Big Ship', the 22-stone Aussie skipper was suffering from a bout of malaria when he went in to bat with his side struggling at 153–5. According to legend, Armstrong cleared his head with a couple of stiff whiskies before scoring an unbeaten century that provided the launch pad for his side's eight-wicket victory.
- **Eddie Paynter (Eng), Brisbane, 1933:** Suffering from acute tonsillitis during the Fourth Test of the Bodyline series, Paynter was ferried off to Brisbane General Hospital where he spent two nights. The following morning local doctors felt Paynter was too ill to take any further part in the match, but as he listened on the radio to the sound of England wickets tumbling, the Lanchashire left hander decided to act. After calling for a taxi, Paynter wrapped himself in his dressing gown and instructed the cab to head for the Gabba. His team-mates were astonished to see him, and even more amazed when Paynter pulled on his pads and went out to bat. Ignoring his fever and concentrating mostly on survival, Paynter was still there at the close, having scored 24 valuable runs in 75 minutes. After a good night's sleep back at the hospital, Paynter returned to the ground in the morning to share an unlikely ninth-wicket stand of 92 with Hedley Verity before he fell for a remarkable 83. Appropriately, in England's second innings, it was the still sick Paynter who hit the match and Ashes winning runs with a full-blooded six.
- **Terry Jenner (Aus), Sydney, 1971:** After being hit on the head by a short ball from John Snow the Aussie tailender had to leave the field. However, he was back at the crease the following morning, and despite still feeling a tad groggy managed to take his score from eight to 30 before being last man out.
- **Rick McCosker (Aus), Melbourne, 1977:** In Australia's first innings of the Centenary Test opener, Rick McCosker was struck in the face by a Bob Willis delivery and was later discovered to

have broken his jaw. With the match delicately poised, he came out to bat at number ten in the second innings with his jaw wired shut. Battling through the pain barrier, McCosker scored 25, adding a vital 54 runs for the ninth wicket with century-maker Rodney Marsh. As Australia eventually won the match by just 45 runs, McCosker's brave innings was probably the difference between victory and defeat.

- **Rick Darling (Aus), Adelaide, 1979:** Struck by a viciously rising Bob Willis delivery, Darling almost died when the gum he was chewing became lodged in his throat. Happily, some emergency first-aid by England's John Emburey revived the Aussie batsman, but a white-faced Darling still had to be stretchered off to the dressing room. Remarkably, he was sufficiently fit to resume his innings the following morning, although he soon fell to Ian Botham.

- **Steve Waugh (Aus), The Oval, 2001:** After pulling a muscle in his left calf earlier in the series, Waugh's tour looked to be over. However, the Aussie skipper insisted on returning for the Fifth Test at The Oval and, despite being far from fully fit, hit 157 not out in his side's innings victory.

— FREDDIE: A FREEMAN OF PRESTON! —

England's 2005 Ashes victory wasn't only celebrated on a national stage in London. Around the country borough councils got in on the act by awarding honours to the local heroes who had sent the Aussies packing. These included:

Andrew Flintoff: Freedom of Preston
Michael Vaughan: Freedom of Sheffield
Ashley Giles: Honorary citizen of Droitwich
Marcus Trescothick: Citizenship award from Taunton Deane Borough

Flintoff was certainly thrilled by his award, saying after England's Ashes triumph: "The most exciting thing is that I'll be awarded the freedom of Preston. That means I can drive a flock of sheep through the town centre, drink for free in no less than 64 pubs, and get a lift home with the police when I'm drunk. What more could you want?" Er, how about your own personal sheepdog, Freddie?

— IN HIS FATHER'S FOOTSTEPS —

Fathers and sons to have figured in Ashes cricket:

England
Fred Tate (1902) and Maurice Tate (1924–30)
Joe Hardstaff snr (1907–08) and Joe Hardstaff jnr (1936–48)
Jeff Jones (1965–66) and Simon Jones (2002–05)
Chris Broad (1986–89) and Stuart Broad (2009–)

Australia
Ned Gregory (1877) and Syd Gregory (1890–1912)

— THE WOMEN'S ASHES —

Women's Test series between England and Australia date back to 1935 but were not officially known as the Ashes until 1998, when an autographed bat was burned before the First Test at Lord's.

Australia held the Ashes for 20 years until England gained a 1–0 series win in 2005, the same year as their male counterparts ended the Aussies' grip on the famous urn. England retained the Ashes two years later Down Under, but Australia got their revenge in 2011, winning a single Test in Sydney by seven wickets.

Country	Years held Ashes
England	1935–49
Australia	1949–1963
England	1963–1985
Australia	1985–2005
England	2005–2011
Australia	2011–

— ASHES LEGENDS: IAN BOTHAM —

One of the greatest all-rounders ever, Ian Botham's aggressive approach to the game lit up numerous Ashes clashes.

Botham made his Test debut aged 21 against the Aussies in 1977, but it was in the 1981 series in England that his match-winning qualities took centre stage. By then, Botham had been promoted to the England captaincy, but he resigned as skipper after 12 Tests which failed to produce a single victory. The final straw came at Lord's in the Second Test against the Australians when Botham picked up a pair.

Freed of the burdens of captaincy, Botham's form was transformed. At Headingley in the Third Test, with England facing almost certain defeat after following on, he played a belligerent innings of 149 not out which set his side up for an improbable victory. Then, at Edgbaston in another match England looked destined to lose, Botham's fast-medium swing bowling ripped the heart out of the Australian batting as he took five wickets for one run in 28 balls. Another bravura performance at Old Trafford in the Fifth Test, where his century included six sixes, cemented Botham's position as one of the country's leading sporting icons. He was rewarded for his heroics with the Man of the Series award and, a few months later, he was voted BBC Sports Personality of the Year – the last cricketer to win the award until Andrew Flintoff in 2005.

Throughout the 1980s, Botham was rarely out of the news. In 1986 he was briefly suspended for smoking cannabis, only to mark his return to the Test arena by taking a wicket with his first ball against New Zealand. "Who writes your scripts?" asked Graham Gooch, as 'Beefy' delivered the perfect response to his detractors.

Beefy lets rip

By the time of his final Test in 1992, Botham had scored over 5,000 runs and taken well in excess of 300 wickets – the first cricketer in history to pass both landmarks. He retired from the first-class game the following year, starting a new career as a commentator.

Away from cricket, Botham has appeared at different times in various guises: as a bustling striker for Scunthorpe United, as a competitive team captain on *A Question of Sport*, as an occasional star of panto, and as a tireless fund-raiser for Leukaemia Research, the blood cancer charity of which he became President in 2004. His charity work and huge contribution to cricket were officially recognised in 2007 when he was awarded a knighthood.

Ian Botham factfile
Born: Heswall, Cheshire, 24 November 1955
County/State: Somerset, Worcestershire, Durham, Queensland
Ashes Tests: 36 (1977–89)
Batting: 1,663 runs (ave 29.18)
Bowling: 148 wickets (ave 27.65)

Others on Botham

"Ian Botham would make a great Aussie."
Former Australian quick **Jeff Thomson**, 1986

"The greatest matchwinner the game has ever known."
Former England captain **Mike Brearley**, 1985

— UNLIKELY INJURIES —

A number of players in Ashes matches have injured themselves in strange circumstances:

- **Billy Barnes:** Having starred in England's dramatic victory in Sydney in 1887, Barnes became involved in an argument with Australian captain Percy McDonnell. Barnes threw a punch that missed its target, and instead smashed into a wall – resulting in an injury that kept the England bowler out of the Second and final Test.
- **Ted Dexter:** In 1965 the England captain was run over by his own Jaguar when the vehicle pinned him to a warehouse door in west London. Dexter broke a leg in the accident and missed that winter's tour to Australia as a result.
- **Terry Alderman:** When England brought up the 400 at Perth in 1982 around two dozen away fans invaded the field in celebration, halting play for a few minutes. One of the fans ran into Alderman,

fielding near the boundary, and he reacted by attempting to rugby tackle his assailant. Alderman succeeded in bringing his man down, but in the process so badly damaged his right shoulder that he missed the rest of the Ashes series.

- **John Crawley:** Returning to the England hotel from a night out in Cairns in November 1998, 'Creepy' Crawley was attacked by a drunk. The batsman's face still bore the scars some days later and although he was declared fit by team manager Graham Gooch, a shaken Crawley was left out of the England side for the First Test in Brisbane.

- **Mark Butcher:** The England batsman had already cricked his neck in a car accident when he damaged his wrist lifting weights in South Africa during the winter of 2004/05. The injury still hadn't cleared up by the summer, so Butcher had to sit out the entire 2005 Ashes series.

- **Glenn McGrath:** Warming up before the Edgbaston Test in 2005, Australia's main strike bowler trod on a stray cricket ball and tore his ankle ligaments. The injury put him out of the match, which England famously won by just two runs.

— 'THE ASHES! IT'S THE ASHES!' —

The 1953 series between England and Australia was one of the closest contests in Ashes history. The first four Tests were all draws, but lacked nothing in drama and excitement. In the First Test at Trent Bridge, for example, Alec Bedser's 14 wickets had appeared to set England on the road to victory, only for the home side to be foiled by the rain as their second innings was cut short on 120–1 with just over one hundred runs required.

In the Second Test at Lord's, however, England were staring defeat in the face until they were rescued by a four and a quarter hour stand between all-rounder Trevor Bailey and century-maker Willie Watson. Millions listened on their radios as the pair defied the Australian bowlers, the match eventually finishing with the tourists three wickets short of victory.

The thrills continued at Old Trafford, where Australia collapsed to 35–8 in their second innings before being saved by the clock. The pendulum swung the other way, though, at Headingley in the Fourth Test where England's bowlers had to resort to defensive tactics to prevent the Australians reaching their victory target of 177 in 115 minutes. All the same, the visitors only fell 30 runs short in another gripping finale.

On, then, to the Fifth and final Test at The Oval which England simply had to win if they were to regain the Ashes after 19 long years of Australian domination. To ensure a result the match was extended to six days but, in the event, only lasted four. Encouraged by sell-out crowds, Len Hutton's team took a stranglehold on the game and, with spinners Jim Laker and Tony Lock dismissing the Aussies cheaply in the second innings, eventually won the match by the convincing margin of eight wickets. As England's star batsman, Denis Compton, swept the winning boundary TV commentator Brian Johnston summed up the joy felt by the country's cricket lovers by excitedly shrieking, 'The Ashes! It's the Ashes!'

Fittingly, the return of the Ashes after nearly two barren decades came in The Queen's Coronation year – a happy coincidence which only added to the festive mood of the nation. The celebrations, though, were somewhat more restrained than the ones which were sparked by England's Ashes triumph in 2005 – as Matthew Engel pointed out in Wisden: "Len Hutton, the victorious Ashes captain 52 years earlier, had to be content with a reception at the Albert Hall. No, not *the* Albert Hall – the Albert Hall, Pudsey. There was, apparently, quite a throng in the martketplace to greet the local hero." How times change . . .

— TEAM OF CROCKS —

England's 1994/95 tour of Australia was a far from happy one as Mike Atherton's side went down to a 3–1 defeat and suffered an appalling run of injuries which wrecked any chance of the team returning with the Ashes.

Indeed, no fewer than six members of the original 16-man squad were forced out of the tour at some stage through injury: Darren Gough (fractured foot), Graeme Hick (slipped disc), Martin McCague (shin stress fracture), Alec Stewart (broken finger), Shaun Udal (torn side muscle) and Craig White (torn side muscle).

In addition to these major injuries, fast bowlers Devon Malcolm and Joey Benjamin went down with chicken pox, while Mike Atherton (bad back), John Crawley (calf), Phil DeFreitas (groin and hamstring) and Graham Thorpe (adductor muscle) also had to seek treatment. Mind you, there was little point knocking on the door of tour physiotherapist Dave Roberts – he joined the ranks of the walking wounded after suffering a broken finger while taking part in a fielding practice session!

— CROWD RECORD —

A record Ashes crowd of 89,155 attended the first day's play of the Melbourne Test on 23 November 2006. The attendance was only 1,645 short of the all-time Test record of 90,800, set at the same ground during the 1960/61 series between Australia and the West Indies.

As on most of the days during the one-sided 2006/07 Ashes series, the Australian fans in the huge crowd enjoyed themselves more than the English ones. Batting first, the visitors were dismissed for just 159 while, in reply, Australia reached 48–2 at stumps.

— ALL CHANGE —

Any English cricketer playing on the county circuit in 1989 had a more than decent chance of performing in the Ashes as, during that summer's series, the England selectors called up a record 29 players for the six-match home series against the Aussies.

Here's a full list of the players selected by England that summer, complete with the number of Tests each appeared in:

6 Tests: David Gower (capt), Jack Russell
5 Tests: Graham Gooch, Robin Smith
4 Tests: -
3 Tests: Kim Barnett, Ian Botham, Nick Cook, Tim Curtis, John Emburey, Neil Foster, Angus Fraser
2 Tests: Mike Atherton, Chris Broad, Graham Dilley, Paul Jarvis, Derek Pringle
1 Test: David Capel, Phil DeFreitas, Mike Gatting, Eddie Hemmings, Alan Igglesden, Allan Lamb, Martyn Moxon, Devon Malcolm, Phil Newport, Tim Robinson, Gladstone Small, John Stephenson, Chris Tavaré

While England handed out caps willy-nilly the Australians, by contrast, only made one change throughout the whole series – seamer Greg Campbell giving way to leg spinner Trevor Hohns after the First Test at Headingley. So, what would prove more successful: the Aussies' settled team or England's 'there's a cricketer, let's pick him!' policy? The away side's crushing 4–0 victory provided a resounding answer.

— AUSTRALIA: BEST ASHES NICKNAME XI —

1. Geoff 'Swampy' Marsh (1986–91)
2. Ricky 'Punter' Ponting (1997–)
3. Donald 'The Don' Bradman (1928–48)
4. Allan 'Captain Grumpy' Border (1979–93)
5. Adam 'The Demolition Man' Gilchrist (2001–07)
6. Richie 'Diamonds' Benaud (1953–63)
7. Kerry 'Skull' O'Keeffe (1971–77)
8. Dennis 'The Menace' Lillee (1971–82)
9. Jason 'Dizzy' Gillespie (1997–2005)
10. Merv 'The Swerve' Hughes (1986–93)
11. Fred 'The Demon' Spofforth (1877–87)

— 'CALL YOURSELF A BATSMAN?' —

Australians are the acknowledged masters of 'sledging', the practice of attempting to put off an opponent with a witty remark or, more often, a barrage of personal abuse. English players have occasionally responded with a well-aimed barb or two or their own, but given their long history in the art of sledging it's no surprise that this list of memorable Ashes putdowns is dominated by Aussies:

"So how's your wife . . . and my kids?"
Australian wicketkeeper **Rod Marsh** to Ian Botham

"We make a good pair, don't we? I can't fucking bat and you can't fucking bowl."
Robin Smith to Merv Hughes after the Aussie bowler had suggested to the English batsman that he was useless. Smith responded by hitting Hughes for six.

"Does your husband play cricket as well?"
Merv Hughes, determined to have the last say in his war of words with Robin Smith

"If the Poms win the toss and bat, keep the taxi running."
Australian fans' banner

"Tufnell! Can I borrow your brain? I'm building an idiot."
Australian fan to **Phil Tufnell**

"If they call me a 'Pommie bastard' or something, I'll say, 'You're right, mate. Now buy me a beer.'"
Phil Tufnell remains unfazed by the brickbats

"Ashes to ashes, dust to dust – if Thomson don't get ya, Lillee must"
Sydney Telegraph cartoon caption, 1974

"I hate bowling at you. I'm not as good at hitting a moving target."
Dennis Lillee to the hyperactive Derek Randall, after Randall's century in the 1977 Centenary Test

"If we don't beat you, we'll knock your bloody heads off."
England fast bowler **Bill Voce** to Australia's Vic Richardson at the start of the Bodyline series, 1932

"They are traitors. They are still Australians. They only did it because they were never going to be good enough to play for Australia."
Shane Warne, criticising Martin McCague and Craig White for deciding to play for England

"You got an MBE, right? For scoring seven at The Oval?"
Shane Warne to Paul Collingwood, during the final Test of the 2006/07 Ashes series

— SUBS IN THE LIMELIGHT —

Gary Pratt is not the only substitute fielder to have made a name for himself in an Ashes Test:

- In the Second Test at Lord's in 1884 England's WG Grace injured a finger while fielding and, in the absence of a twelfth man, was replaced by Australia captain Billy Murdoch who proceeded to catch team-mate Henry 'Tup' Scott – the first instance of a dismissal by a sub fielder in the history of Test cricket. Presumably, Scott, who was going well on 75 when he was snapped up by Murdoch, was not first in line to buy his skipper a drink at the close of play.
- In the Second Test at Sydney in 1887 Australian fast bowler Charles 'The Terror' Turner took a sub catch for England to dismiss debutant Reginald Allen for 30 in the home side's second innings. *The Sydney Morning Herald* described Turner's effort as a 'very smart catch' and it helped England clinch a series-winning victory by 71 runs.
- In the First Test in 1930 England recruited Sydney Copley from the Trent Bridge groundstaff to field in place of Harold Larwood, who was suffering from a stomach upset. Chasing 429 to win, Australia were well-placed at 229–3 until Copley held on to a superb diving catch at mid on to dismiss Stan McCabe. The great Don Bradman followed soon afterwards and England won the

match by 93 runs. "Stan played it hard and low not more than six inches off the ground," recalled Copley years later. "I made many yards to reach it and with a terrific effort I seized the ball and turned a somersault, still clinging to the ball, to break up a dangerous partnership. I was picked off the ground by a very jubilant captain."

- In the Second Test of the 1989 series a member of the Lord's groundstaff, Robert Sims, caught Australia captain Allan Border at long leg off the bowling of Neil Foster. However, the dismissal made little difference to the result of the match, which was won by Australia by six wickets.

— VANDALS SCUPPER ENGLAND'S ASHES CHANCES —

1–0 down after two Tests, England had a great chance of levelling the 1975 Ashes series in the Third Test at Headingley. Having set Australia 445 to win, the tourists were 220–3 at the close of play on the fourth day, with opener Rick McCosker 95 not out. All three results were still possible, but if England could make an early breakthrough on the final day a home victory would be very much on the cards.

Except there was no play on the fifth day – and, for once, the English weather was not to blame. The first sign that all was not well was the appearance of graffiti claiming that 'George Davis is innocent' on the walls surrounding the ground. The slogan was a familiar one, campaigners protesting the innocence of convicted armed robber Davis having daubed it at numerous sites around the country.

The real shock, though, came when head groundsman George Cawthray inspected his pitch. To his horror, it had been dug up with knives and gallons of oil had been poured in the holes. "When I first saw the damage it did not sink in," he recalled. "I was amazed. I thought I should be able to repair the holes but it was the oil that did the damage."

Captains Tony Greig and Ian Chappell agreed that the pitch was unplayable and, to the disappointment of fans across the world, an intriguingly poised Test was abandoned as a draw, guaranteeing that Australia would retain the Ashes.

Four people were later tried for digging up the pitch, three of them receiving suspended sentences and one, Peter Chappell (no relation to the Aussie skipper!), an 18-month prison sentence. As for Davis, he was released from Albany Prison on the Isle of Wight the following year after Home Secretary Roy Jenkins ruled that there were grave doubts about the police evidence in his case. However, in July 1978 east Londoner Davis was jailed for 15 years after pleading guilty to taking part in a bank robbery. England fans must have wished that he had entered the same plea at his earlier trial!

— ASHES LEGENDS: STEVE WAUGH —

The most-capped player in Test history, Steve Waugh was a pivotal figure in the Australian side which dominated the Ashes in the 1990s and into the new millennium.

Selected for the Aussies originally as an all-rounder, Waugh entered a team at a low ebb and experienced Ashes defeat in 1986/87. His country's fortunes began to revive, however, with victory in the 1987 World Cup, a triumph in which Waugh played a full part. Two years later, in 1989, his batting at last realised its potential with a first Test century against England at Headingley.

Following a run of poor form in 1991, Waugh was dropped from the Australian side and replaced by his minutes-younger twin brother, Mark. This setback was only temporary, though, as Steve was recalled to the team after remodelling his batting style, focusing primarily on defence while waiting for the loose ball to punish. He also developed an effective 'slog sweep' shot against spin bowling, a stroke which brought him many runs in the ensuing years.

A pair of centuries at Old Trafford in 1997 emphasised how important Waugh was to the Australian team, even if a longstanding back problem reduced his impact as a bowler. Two years later, in 1999, Waugh took over the captaincy following the retirement of Mark Taylor. He proved to be an immensely successful skipper, winning 41 of the 57 Tests in which he performed coin-tossing duties and maintaining Australia's stranglehold on the Ashes. Under his leadership, the Aussies not only beat but frequently outclassed the opposition, and were hailed as the country's best team since Bradman's Invincibles.

Waugh's last series against England was in 2002/03. Under pressure from the Australian media after suffering a dip in form, Waugh responded by hitting a chanceless century in the Fifth Test at Sydney, reaching his ton with a four off the last ball of the day. He left the ground to a standing ovation, and the occasion was later dubbed Steve Waugh's 'Perfect Day'. The following year he played his last Test innings against India, receiving a salute from the ferries in Sydney Harbour when he reached fifty in the second innings.

A keen photographer, Waugh is also a firm supporter of charitable causes, notably a children's leper colony in Calcutta. Partly because of his charity work he was voted Australian of the Year in 2004, and in 2005 he was named Australian Father of the Year.

Steve Waugh factfile
Born: Canterbury, New South Wales, 2 June 1965
State: New South Wales
County: Kent, Somerset
Ashes Tests: 46 (1986–2003)
Batting: 3,200 runs (ave 58.18)
Bowling: 22 wickets (ave 41.55)

Others on Waugh

"A man for every occasion and perhaps the most ruthless cricketer I've ever played with."
Shane Warne

"With the possible exception of Rolf Harris, no other Australian has inflicted more pain and grief on Englishmen since Don Bradman."
Mike Walters in *The Daily Mirror*

— THE BOWLING WICKETKEEPER —

In the 1884 Test at The Oval, Australia's first innings took up an incredible 311 (four ball) overs. This was in the days before declarations, which weren't permitted until 1889, so England's only option was to bowl the visitors out – however long it took.

Seeking to give some variety to his attack, England captain Lord Harris called on all his fielders to bowl some overs. Then, in a last desperate measure to dismiss the Aussies, Harris handed the ball to wicketkeeper Alfred Lyttleton. The plan worked a treat as Lyttleton proceeded to take 4–19 with lobs while still wearing his pads!

The wicketkeeper's success, though, was not such a great surprise as he was a noted all-round sportsman, who had scored for England in his one international football appearance against Scotland in 1877. Lyttleton, a professional lawyer who was a nephew of William Gladstone, later became an MP, serving in the House of Commons from 1895 until his death in 1913.

— BRADMAN'S DUCK —

On 14 August 1948 Don Bradman strode out of the Oval pavilion, receiving a standing ovation from the crowd and the England team. It was the Don's final innings for his country and, following a superb unbeaten 173 in the previous Test at Headingley, he needed just four runs to clinch an unprecedented Test average of 100.

However, facing journeyman leg-break bowler Eric Hollies, Bradman was out for a second-ball duck, falling to a googly that beat his forward push and bowled him between bat and pad. "It's not easy to bat with tears in your eyes," said Bradman afterwards, suggesting that his concentration was not what it might have been. However, England wicketkeeper Godfrey Evans was not convinced by Bradman's explanation for his early departure. "I didn't see any tears, and I was standing behind the stumps, right up close," he recalled.

Tears or no tears, Bradman's duck knocked his Test average down to 99.94. There was some consolation for the master batsman, though, as he was given another emotional ovation as he left the Test arena for the last time. Not that Hollies was too impressed. "My best bloody ball of the season," he complained to a fielder, "and they're clapping *him*."

— MADCAP TUFNELL IS OVAL KING —

During Australia's domination of the Ashes in the 1990s, England had to be content with the occasional Test win – and hope that the next series would bring better luck. One of England's most famous victories during this bleak period came at The Oval in 1997, with spinner Phil Tufnell putting in a Man of the Match performance with figures of 11–93.

The game, though, began disappointingly for England, who were trailing 3–1 in the series and had already waved goodbye to any chance of reclaiming the Ashes. Dismissed in their first innings for 180 the home side looked to be in severe trouble, but Tufnell came to the rescue with 7–66 as the Aussies were bowled out for 220. However, England batted poorly again in their second innings, with only Mark Butcher (13), Graham Thorpe (62) and Mark Ramprakash (48) making double figures in another low total of just 163. Set 124 to win, the Australians were hot favorites, but Tufnell (4–27) and fast bowler Andy Caddick (5–42) put in heroic displays as England scraped home by 19 runs.

For Tufnell, in particular, victory tasted sweet as he had controversially been left out of the five previous Tests. Possibly, the selectors were wary of picking a player who had a reputation as a maverick and, during the previous Ashes series in Australia, had smashed up a hotel room while struggling to cope with personal problems. After this incident, Tufnell was sent for psychiatric examination in a Perth hospital. The bowler soon discharged himself, recalling later: "I was sitting there in a hospital with some bloke shining a light in my eyes and saying, 'Tell me about your childhood,' and I just thought to myself, 'What the hell am I doing here? This is ridiculous!'"

— RUNS IN SHORT SUPPLY —

The fewest runs scored in a full day's play of Ashes cricket is 106 by England at Brisbane in 1958. Peter May's team started the fourth day on 92–2 and by the time the eighth wicket fell five minutes before the close had advanced snail-like to 198–8.

The chief culprit for the slow rate of scoring was Trevor 'The Boil' Bailey whose innings of 68 was tortuously compiled from 425 deliveries (including 385 'dot' balls). Despite Bailey's valiant – but, from a spectator's point of view, really rather tedious – rearguard action, England still lost the Test by eight wickets.

— ARISE, SIR PELHAM! —

The eight Ashes cricketers to have been knighted are:

Player	Year knighted
Sir Pelham Warner (Eng, 1903–12)	1937
Sir Donald Bradman (Aus, 1928–48)	1949
Sir Jack Hobbs (Eng, 1908–30)	1953
Sir Len Hutton (Eng, 1938–55)	1956
Sir George 'Gubby' Allen (Eng, 1930–37)	1986
Sir Colin Cowdrey (Eng, 1954–75)	1992
Sir Alec Bedser (Eng, 1946–54)	1996
Sir Ian Botham (Eng, 1977–89)	2007

— PROLIFIC CENTURIONS —

Aussie great Don Bradman holds the record for the most Ashes hundreds, with 19 tons to his name – a total no other batsman can match in Tests between two countries. 'The Don' notched his first century against England at Melbourne in 1929 and raised his bat for the last time when he hit 173 not out at Headingley in 1948. For England, Jack Hobbs is the most regular century maker in Ashes Tests, with 12.

Player	Centuries	Highest score
Don Bradman (Aus)	19	334 at Headingley, 1930
Jack Hobbs (Eng)	12	187 at Adelaide, 1912
Steve Waugh (Aus)	10	177* at Headingley, 1989
Greg Chappell (Aus)	9	144 at Sydney, 1975
David Gower (Eng)	9	215 at Edgbaston, 1985
Wally Hammond (Eng)	9	251 at Sydney, 1928/29
Allan Border (Aus)	8	200* at Headingley, 1993
Arthur Morris (Aus)	8	206 at Adelaide, 1951
Ricky Ponting (Aus)	8	196 at Brisbane, 2006
Herbert Sutcliffe (Eng)	8	194 at Sydney, 1932

* not out

— THE GREAT ASHES SERIES: A NEW ERA DAWNS, ENGLAND 1989 —

Having held the Ashes for all but two of the previous 12 years, England began this series as favourites. However, the bookies were soon readjusting their odds after Australia passed the 600 mark in their first innings, opener Mark Taylor helping himself to a century on his debut and Steve Waugh chipping in with an unbeaten ton lower down the order. England, aided by a magnificent century from Allan Lamb, posted a decent total in reply but collapsed in their second innings after the Aussies had set David Gower's side a victory target of 402. Seam bowler Terry Alderman inflicted the most damage on the home team, taking ten wickets in the match.

Australia continued their dominance at Lord's, taking a big first innings lead. On the evening of the third day, with England in dire trouble at 58–3 in their second innings, a rattled Gower stormed out of a press conference claiming he had to catch a taxi to a West End theatre. Despite a century from the skipper and 96 from Robin Smith on the fourth day, England couldn't prevent the Aussies from winning by six wickets.

England again struggled at Edgbaston, but were saved from further humiliation by a combination of rain and bad light. The established pattern, however, was renewed at Old Trafford where Australia cruised to a nine-wicket victory and so regained the Ashes for the first time on English soil since 1934.

By the time of the Fifth Test at Trent Bridge, England were in a shambolic state. Throughout the summer the selectors had wrung the changes to little positive effect, and another new-look side, featuring debutants Mike Atherton and Devon Malcolm, fared just as poorly as their predecessors. Aussie openers Geoff Marsh (138) and Mark Taylor

(219) batted throughout the first day, going on to share an Ashes record stand for the first wicket as Allan Border's men again hit the 600 mark. In reply, England were twice dismissed cheaply and went down limply to their biggest ever home defeat against Australia.

The agony continued at The Oval, where England narrowly avoided the follow on and were only saved from another probable defeat by Border's bizarre decision to delay his declaration until lunch on the final day.

Even so, the series could only be described as a rout. The Australians' ability to post big scores quickly – so putting their opponents under huge pressure when it was their turn to bat – was the key to their success, and would become a feature of their play over the next 15 years, during which they would dominate not just England but every other Test-playing country in the world.

First Test: Headingley, June 8–13
Australia 601–7 dec & 230–3 dec, England 430 & 191
Australia won by 210 runs

Second Test: Lord's, June 22–27
England 286 & 359, Australia 528 & 119–4
Australia won by six wickets

Third Test: Edgbaston, July 6–11
Australia 424 & 158–2, England 242
Match drawn

Fourth Test: Old Trafford, July 27–Aug 1
England 260 & 264, Australia 447 & 81–1
Australia won by nine wickets

Fifth Test: Trent Bridge, Aug 10–14
Australia 602–6 dec, England 255 & 167
Australia won by an innings and 180 runs

Sixth Test: The Oval, Aug 24–29
Australia 468 & 219–4 dec, England 285 & 143–5
Match drawn

Star performers

For England: Middle order batsman Robin Smith (ave 61.44) was the only home player to get the measure of the Aussie bowlers.

For Australia: Steve Waugh and Mark Taylor were the pick of the batsmen, while Terry Alderman's haul of 41 wickets was just one short of his 1981 record.

They said it

"I'm not aware of any mistakes I have made."
Ted Dexter, chairman of selectors, after picking 29 players for England in six Tests

"We have a bit of rebuilding to do and we need some continuity. To throw everything up in the air, including the captaincy, would not be helpful."
David Gower, who nonetheless was replaced as England captain after the series by Graham Gooch

— BODYLINE: THE TV SERIES —

In 1984 the notorious Bodyline Ashes series of 1932/33 was the subject of an Australian TV mini-series, appropriately enough called *Bodyline*. Spanning 330 minutes and seven episodes, the series' pro-Aussie and anti-English leanings were not disguised – after all, a production that melodramatically billed itself as 'the day England declared war on Australia' could not be confused with a balanced and impartial take on events.

Nonetheless, the series was a hit in England as well as Australia and earned praise from reviewers for its vivid recreation of the most famous of Ashes clashes. The cast list included:

Actor	Character
Gary Sweet	Don Bradman (Aus)
Hugo Weaving	Douglas Jardine (Eng)
John Walton	Bert Woodfull (Aus)
Jim Holt	Harold Larwood (Eng)
Les Dayman	Bert Oldfield (Aus)
John Doyle	George 'Gubby' Allen (Eng)
Michael Winchester	Stan McCabe (Aus)

For those who missed it, here's a snatch of typical dialogue from *Bodyline*:
Heckler (on a small boat alongside the England ship as it arrives in Australia): "Go home, you Pommie bastards! You don't stand a chance against Bradman!"
Douglas Jardine (on deck to his players): "Gentlemen, we are entering the land of the barbarian."

— A LOAD OF BALLS —

These days, Ashes Tests in both England and Australia are played with six-ball overs, but the number of balls per over has not always been standardised north and south of the Equator. Starting with maiden-friendly four-ball overs at the First Test in Melbourne in 1877, the structure of the over in Ashes clashes has altered in the following way:

In England		In Australia	
Years	Balls per Over	Years	Balls per over
1880–1888	4	1877–1887/88	4
1890–1899	5	1891/92–1920/21	6
1902–onwards	6	1924/25	8
		1928/29–1932/33	6
		1936/37–1978/79	8
		1979/80–onwards	6

— ASHES JINX —

Although he was a fine, aggressive batsman who averaged a thoroughly respectable 39.77 in Ashes tests, the last name England fans wanted to see on the teamsheet in the late 1980s and early 1990s was that of Robin Smith. The reason? Well, in his 15 appearances against the Aussies Smith failed to finish on the winning side even once (11 losses, four draws), making him by some distance the unluckiest player in the long history of the Ashes.

For Australia, spinner Ray Bright was a similar 'Jonah' figure for a while, with no wins in his eight Ashes tests (five losses, three draws) between 1977–81. Like Smith, though, Bright could console himself with the thought that he didn't perform at all badly on an individual level, taking 17 wickets at an average of 31.58.

— RECALL OF THE OLD CODGERS —

A number of players have been surprisingly recalled for Ashes action at an advanced age and, for the most part, they have given a good account of themselves:

- **Wilfred Rhodes:** The legendary all-rounder, who made his Ashes debut in 1899 just as WG Grace was bowing out of Test cricket, made his first appearance for England for five years in the final Test at the Oval in 1926. Batting at number seven, Rhodes hit 28 and 14, but it was with the ball that the 48-year-old really shone.

After taking two wickets in Australia's first innings, Rhodes' 4–44 in the second was instrumental in England's 289-run victory which clinched a 1–0 series win for the home side.

- **Freddie Brown:** A former England captain, Freddie Brown was winding down his career in 1953 with Northampton when, as chairman of England's selectors, he decided to pick himself for the Second Test at Lord's against Australia. Brown, 42, acquitted himself well in the drawn game, scoring 50 runs and taking four wickets, but left himself out for the remainder of the series.

- **Cyril Washbrook:** An England batting hero whose opening partnerships with Len Hutton had frustrated many an Aussie bowler, Washbrook became an England selector in 1956. That same year, with England one down in the series, Washbrook was asked to leave the room by his fellow selectors as they discussed the team for the forthcoming Third Test at Headingley. When he returned to the room, the 41-year-old Lancashire legend was asked if he fancied making a return to the England side after an absence of five years. Washbrook accepted the offer, but might have regretted his decision when he found himself joining skipper Peter May in the middle with England in dire trouble at 17–3. "I've never felt so glad in my life as when I saw who was coming in," remarked May later, and together the pair turned England's fortunes around with a magnificent fourth wicket stand of 187. Sadly, Cyril just missed out on a century, falling for 98, but his innings was a crucial factor in England's eventual victory by an innings and 42 runs.

- **Colin Cowdrey:** After injuries to batsmen Dennis Amiss and John Edrich, former England skipper Cowdrey was flown out to Oz as cover for the remainder of the 1974/75 tour Down Under. Never a whippet between the wickets, the rotund Cowdrey was by now waddling his singles, but the 41-year-old still managed to make 22 and, opening the batting, 41 in the Second Test in Perth. After that, though, Cowdrey found the pace of fiery Aussie bowlers Dennis Lillee and Jeff Thomson as difficult to handle as the other England batsman, and ended up averaging just 18.33 in his nine Test innings.

— ASHES LEGENDS: GLENN MCGRATH —

No fast bowler has taken more Test wickets than Glenn McGrath, a key figure in Australia's domination of international cricket during the 1990s and into the new millennium.

When McGrath was growing up in Narromine, New South Wales, however, there was little to suggest that the tall, skinny youngster would one day rewrite the record books. Indeed, his local captain thought so little of his bowling that he refused to give McGrath a bowl. But former Australian all-rounder Doug Walters spotted his potential and, after just eight state matches, McGrath was given his Test debut against New Zealand in 1993.

After a shaky start, the six-foot six-inch paceman soon emerged as the best fast bowler of his generation. Other bowlers may have been faster, but none could match McGrath's immaculate length, unerring accuracy or his ability to generate steep bounce. A glut of wickets followed, the Australian legend claiming his 500th Test victim when he dismissed England opener Marcus Trescothick at Lord's in the 2005 Ashes series.

Famously, McGrath missed the following Test at Edgbaston after injuring his ankle when he stepped on a stray ball in the outfield during practice. Australia lost that Test, and also went down at Trent Bridge when McGrath was again absent, this time with a shoulder problem.

It was surely no coincidence that England achieved their best results of the summer when McGrath was missing. Over the years, the Aussie bowler averaged over five wickets per game against England, playing a major part in Australia's Ashes triumphs up until his retirement from Test cricket in 2007.

Before a number of Ashes series, McGrath had irritated English players and fans with his cocky predictions of an Australian whitewash. Remarkably, in his final Test series, he was spot on as the Aussies trounced Freddie Flintoff's underperforming tourists 5–0 in 2006/07. As so often in the past, McGrath's metronomic line and length proved a valuable weapon and his 21 wickets in the series pushed his final Ashes haul up to 157 – a figure only surpassed by fellow Aussies Shane Warne and Dennis Lillee.

Since his retirement, McGrath has had more time to enjoy his hobby, hunting wild pigs. He is also a keen cook and recently revealed his favourite recipes in *The Glenn McGrath Barbecue Cookbook*.

Glenn McGrath factfile
Born: Dubbo, New South Wales, 9 February 1970
State: New South Wales
County: Middlesex, Worcestershire

Ashes Tests: 30 (1994–2007)
Batting: 103 runs (ave 6.06)
Bowling: 157 wickets (ave 20.93)

Others on McGrath

"He always has the batsmen under pressure and does the basics very well. He is a pest in the changing room but he is good value."
Shane Warne

"He borders on being obsessive compulsive. He knows every Test wicket he's ever taken, how the batsman was out and what number victim they were."
Steve Waugh

— BOGEY GROUND —

Incredibly, until Andrew Strauss' side triumphed in 2009 by 115 runs, England had not beaten Australia at Lord's since 1934, when spinner Hedley Verity took 15 wickets on a rain-affected pitch in the home side's crushing victory by an innings and 38 runs. In the years that followed the Aussies enjoyed nine wins at the home of cricket while remaining undefeated in 18 Tests. Here are the details of the visitors' amazing Lord's run:

Year	Result	Year	Result
1938	Match drawn	1977	Match drawn
1948	Australia won by 409 runs	1980	Match drawn
1953	Match drawn	1981	Match drawn
1956	Australia won by 185 runs	1985	Australia won by 4 wickets
1961	Australia won by 5 wickets	1989	Australia won by 6 wickets
1964	Match drawn	1993	Australia won by an innings and 62 runs
1968	Match drawn	1997	Match drawn
1972	Australia won by 8 wickets	2001	Australia won by 8 wickets
1975	Match drawn	2005	Australia won by 239 runs

Happily for home fans, the Lord's hoodoo finally came to an end in 2009. For once, England started well under the watchful eye of Old Father Time, skipper Strauss (161) and Alastair Cook (95) putting on 196 for the first wicket, before a batting collapse meant they were only able to post a score in excess of 400 after a last-wicket stand of 47 between Jimmy Anderson and Graham Onions. Anderson then starred with the ball, taking four wickets as Australia succumbed for just 215. England decided against enforcing the follow on and, batting for a second time, made 311–6 declared thanks in part to a quick-fire 61 off just 42 balls by wicketkeeper Matt Prior. Set an unlikely 522 to win, Australia looked down and out at 128–5 before Michael Clarke (136) and Brad Haddin (80) raised the tourists' hopes with a sixth-wicket stand of 185. Man of the Match Andrew Flintoff, who had announced his impending retirement from Test cricket before the start of the game, eventually made the breakthrough by dismissing Haddin and then wrapped up the tail to secure a first home win at Lord's against the Aussies for 75 years.

— KEV'S BUTTERFINGERS —

Kevin Pietersen's aggressive batting made him one of England's stars in the epic Ashes series of 2005. Shame about his catching, though. The flamboyant Hampshire star's inability to pocket even the simplest of chances in the field contributed to England's eventual victory being much more nerve-wracking than it might otherwise have been. During the five-match series Pieterson spilled no fewer than six easy catches; the Aussie players to benefit being:

Player	Score when dropped Test (fielding position)	by Pietersen	Score when out
Ricky Ponting	Lord's	3 (fourth slip)	9
Brett Lee	Lord's	3 (gully)	3
Michael Clarke	Lord's	21 (short extra cover)	91
Adam Gilchrist	Old Trafford	12 (cover)	30
Shane Warne	Old Trafford	30 (short midwicket)	34
Michael Kasprowicz	Trent Bridge	19 (midwicket)	19

Happily for England, Pietersen's boobs didn't prove too costly as the reprieved Aussie batsmen only added an average of 17 runs before making their way back to the pavilion.

— A PAIR OF KING PAIRS —

Only two players have recorded a king pair in Ashes matches. The first was England tailender William Attewell, who landed two first-ball ducks in the 1892 Test in Sydney. Thanks partly to Attewell's inept performance with the bat, England lost the Test by 72 runs.

Well over a century later, Australia's Ryan Harris suffered the same fate in the 2010 Brisbane Test. In the first innings he was trapped lbw first ball by Graeme Swann, and second time round he was dismissed in an identical manner by Jimmy Anderson. Harris's failure to trouble the scorers hardly helped the Aussie cause but was rather in keeping with a poor performance by the home side, England cruising to victory by an innings inside four days.

— RODNEY'S NINE VICTIMS —

As well as being the most successful wicketkeeper in Ashes history, Rodney Marsh also holds the record for the number of dismissals in an England-Australia match, with nine in the Brisbane Test of November-December 1982. In England's first innings, Marsh caught Allan Lamb, Geoff Miller and Norman Cowans, all off the bowling of paceman Geoff Lawson. In the second innings, Marsh did even better, taking a further six catches to dismiss Chris Tavaré, Graeme Fowler, David Gower, Ian Botham, Miller and Cowans. Thanks in no small part to Marsh's handiwork behind the stumps, Australia went on to win the game by seven wickets.

In the 2006/07 Ashes series Marsh's record was equalled by Australian wicketkeeper Adam Gilchrist. 'The Demolition Man' lived up to his nickname in the Fifth Test at Sydney by taking five catches in England's first innings and adding a further four dismissals (three catches and a stumping) in the second.

— THE DON LEADS THE WAY —

No prizes for guessing the identity of the batsman who has scored more runs in an Ashes series than any other. Yes, it's that Australian run-machine Don Bradman, who fell just 26 runs short of the 1,000 mark in the 1930 series in England. Bradman also tops the scoring charts for an Australian Down Under, his 810 runs in 1936/37 helping the Aussies fight back from two down to win the series 3–2.

England's most prolific batsman in an Ashes series is the legendary Wally Hammond, whose 905 runs in Australia in 1928/29 were a vital factor in the away side's emphatic 4–1 series victory. Meanwhile, elegant left-hander David Gower is England's highest scorer on home soil with 732 runs, including a personal best 215 at Edgbaston in the Fifth Test, during the Ashes series of 1985.

Player	Year	Venue	Tests	Runs	HS	Ave
Don Bradman (Aus)	1930	England	5	974	334	139.14
Wally Hammond (Eng)	1928/29	Australia	5	905	251	113.12
Mark Taylor (Aus)	1989	England	6	839	219	83.90
Don Bradman (Aus)	1936/37	Australia	5	810	270	90.00
Alastair Cook (Eng)	2010/11	Australia	5	766	235*	127.66
Don Bradman (Aus)	1934	England	5	758	304	94.75
Herbert Sutcliffe (Eng)	1924/25	Australia	5	734	176	81.56
David Gower (Eng)	1985	England	6	732	215	81.33

*not out

— ASHES LEGENDS: SHANE WARNE —

With his peroxide hair, dazzling earrings and chubby physique, Shane Warne always looked more like a Sydney nightclub owner than an international cricketer. But appearances can be deceptive: in the view of many, Warne was quite simply the greatest bowler in the history of Test cricket.

His early playing years, though, did not suggest that greatness was around the corner. Expelled from the Australian Academy for his love of nightlife in 1991, Warne bowled poorly on his Test debut the following year, taking 1–228 against India. The selectors persevered with the young leg spinner, however, and he rewarded their patience with some outstanding performances – many of them against England.

In 1993, Warne announced his arrival on the Ashes scene by dismissing Mike Gatting with his first ball, a delivery that spun eighteen inches outside leg stump to clip off. In the space of a few seconds a star was born, and Warne cemented his reputation throughout the summer by bewildering his opponents with the full extent of his repertoire: top spinners, back spinners, flippers, sliders and zooters.

The following year in Melbourne, Warne became the first bowler since 1903 to take a hat-trick in an Ashes Test. Perhaps, though, his finest displays against England came in 2005 when he claimed 40 wickets in the series despite finishing on the losing side, along the way passing Dennis Lillee's old record of 167 Ashes wickets. Two years later he announced his retirement from Test cricket after taking another 23 wickets in Australia's stunning 2006/07 Ashes series victory.

Warne's incredible achievements were recognized in 2000 when a panel of experts selected him as one of the five Wisden Cricketers of the Century. Always popular in England despite his Ashes successes, Warne was also voted the BBC Overseas Sports Personality of the Year in 2005.

Less happily, Warne has been involved in a number of scandals. In 1998 he admitted receiving £3,000 from an Indian bookmaker in exchange for information about pitch conditions. The revelation probably cost him the Australian captaincy. Then, in 2003, Warne was banned from cricket for a year after failing a drugs test. In his defence, he claimed his mother had given him a 'fluid tablet' to help him lose his double chin. Lurid tabloid headlines also followed when Warne was accused of sending saucy text messages to a string of women.

"Bowled Warney!"

Amazingly, none of these incidents ever seemed to affect Warne's form. If anything, his bowling became even more clever and subtle as the years passed. One of the greatest players and biggest characters to grace international cricket, his departure from the Test scene has left a huge void.

Shane Warne factfile
Born: Ferntree Gully, Victoria, 13 September 1968
State: Victoria
County: Hampshire
Ashes Tests: 36 (1993–2007)
Batting: 1,134 runs (ave 23.62)
Bowling: 195 wickets (ave 23.25)

Others on Warne

"He's just a genius. He's a one-off."
England batsman **Kevin Pietersen**

"Shane's ability to dismiss all types of batsmen in a variety of conditions marks him as one of the greatest bowlers in cricket's history."
Bob Merriman, chairman of Cricket Australia, paying tribute to Warne after he took his 500th Test wicket in 2004

— GOWER LEADS FROM THE FRONT—

The burdens of captaincy have often left Ashes skippers struggling for form with bat or ball – Ricky Ponting being a prime example during the recent 2010/11 series – but this certainly wasn't the case when David Gower led England during the 1985 home series against Australia.

Appointed captain two years earlier, Gower was in splendid form throughout the series and was a key figure as England regained the Ashes with a well-deserved 3–1 victory. A win apiece in the opening two Tests at Headingley and Lord's was followed by a high-scoring draw at Trent Bridge, Gower scoring a magnificent 166 in England's first innings. Another draw followed at Old Trafford, leaving the series to be decided in the final two Tests.

In the Fifth Test at Edgbaston, Australia posted a reasonable-looking score of 335 but it was made to look wholly inadequate as England responded with 595–5 declared, Gower compiling a marvellous double century full of exquisite strokes. In their second innings the Aussies were dismissed for just 142, swing bowler Richard Ellison taking four wickets to claim 10–104 in the match, and England won by the crushing margin of an innings and 118 runs.

Australia needed to win at The Oval to square the series and hold on to the Ashes, but they were again trounced in similar fashion. Once more Gower was in superb form, hitting 157 in breezy style and together with Graham Gooch (196) was mainly responsible for England's impressive first innings score of 464. The demoralised Aussies only managed 241 in reply and, after Gower had enforced the follow on, collapsed to 129 all out with Ellison taking another five wickets.

While England's success had been a team effort, there was no doubt that captain Gower was the star of the series. His total of 732 runs (at an average of 81.33) remains a record for an English batsman in a home series, while his three centuries were each mini-masterpieces, scored with the seemingly effortless brilliance that was the Gower trademark.

Happily for England, Gower's purple patch continued on the 1986/87 tour of Australia, where he averaged nearly 58 as Mike Gatting's side retained the Ashes with a 2–1 series victory. By the time his England career ended in 1992, the curly-haired Leicestershire left-hander had written himself into the Ashes record books with a total of 3,269 runs against the Aussies (a figure only surpassed by Jack Hobbs) including nine centuries (again, only Hobbs with 12 has scored more).

— OUCH! THAT HURT . . . —

The last ten batsmen to retire hurt in Ashes cricket are:

Player	Year	Venue	Score
Justin Langar (Aus)	2001	The Oval	102
Steve Waugh (Aus)	2001	Trent Bridge	1
Nasser Hussain (Eng)	2001	Edgbaston	9
John Dyson (Aus)	1982	Brisbane	4
Garth McKenzie (Aus)	1971	Sydney	6
Bill Lawry (Aus)	1968	Edgbaston	6
Barry Jarman (Aus)	1968	Lord's	0
Norm O'Neill (Aus)	1964	Trent Bridge	24
Syd Barnes (Aus)	1948	Old Trafford	1
Len Hutton (Eng)	1947	Sydney	122

As you can see, the list is dominated by Australians – so much for their popular reputation as macho tough guys who never flinch under fire!

— ON THE BOX —

A selection of non-cricket related TV appearances by Ashes players past and present:

Mike Atherton: as himself, *Trevor's World of Sport* (BBC, 2003)

Ian Botham: team captain, *A Question of Sport* (BBC, 1988–96); presenter, *Athletes Behaving Badly* (ITV, 2002)

Mike Gatting: as himself, *Trevor's World of Sport* (BBC, 2003)

Darren Gough: winner with Lilia Kopylova, *Strictly Come Dancing* (BBC, 2005); guest captain, *A Question of Sport* (BBC, 2007)

David Gower: team captain, *They Think It's All Over* (BBC, 1995–2003); competitor, *Celebrity, Ready Steady Cook* (BBC, 2001); as himself, *Trevor's World of Sport* (BBC, 2003); contributor, *Grumpy Old Men* (BBC, 2003)

Mark Ramprakash: winner with Karen Hardy, *Strictly Come Dancing* (BBC, 2006)

Fred Trueman: actor, *Dad's Army* (BBC, 1970); presenter, *Indoor League* (ITV, 1973); team captain, *A Question of Sport* (BBC, 1976)

Phil Tufnell: winner, *I'm a Celebrity, Get Me Out of Here!* (ITV, 2003); team captain, *They Think It's All Over* (BBC, 2003–05); presenter, *Simply the Best* (ITV, 2004); reporter, *The One Show* (BBC, 2007)

Shane Warne: as himself, *Neighbours* (BBC, 2006); guest captain, *A Question of Sport* (BBC, 2007)

— THE 1896 PLAYERS' STRIKE —

The 1896 Ashes series was in the balance at 1–1 when five England players threatened not to play in the deciding Test at The Oval. The players' gripe was over match fees, and was fuelled by the preferential treatment of England captain WG Grace.

England's leading professionals suspected that Grace, who had just enjoyed a bumper £9,073 testimonial with his county, Gloucestershire, was receiving far more than the standard match fee of £10 per game. So, on the eve of the match at The Oval, five players – Bobby Abel, Billy Gunn, Tom Hayward, George Lohmann and Tom Richardson – demanded a fee of £20. Four of the players were on Surrey's staff and might have imagined that their county club, as the organisers of the Test, would be sympathetic to their case. However, the players' demands were flatly refused and the strike was on.

On the morning of the match, though, Abel, Hayward and Richardson backed down, agreeing to play in the match for the normal fee. But Nottinghamshire batsman Gunn and Surrey fast bowler Lohmann stuck to their guns, refusing to take to the field.

The strikers were not missed. England won a rain-affected, low-scoring match by 66 runs, dismissing Australia for just 44 in their second innings. Predictably, the cricket establishment adopted an unforgiving attitude towards the pair of rebels: Lohmann was never selected for England again, while Gunn had to wait three years before he was recalled to international duty.

— FREDDIE DRINKS FOR ENGLAND —

England's 2005 Ashes heroes celebrated their historic triumph in style by running up a bar bill of £34,000 at their team hotel near Tower Bridge. Much of the booze went down the neck of Man of the Series Andrew Flintoff, who drank his team-mates under the table in a marathon 21-hour binge. Here are the details of Freddie's extraordinary drinking session:

Monday
6.30pm: Champagne and beer in The Oval dressing-room.
8pm-midnight: Beers back at the team hotel.

Tuesday
Midnight-4am: While other members of the team head out to Soho, Flintoff knocks back gin and tonics at the hotel bar.
4am-7am: Freddie stays awake by gulping down refreshing cranberry juice – laced with lashings of vodka.
7am: Breakfast. Flintoff passes on the customary tea and toast, ordering beer instead.
8am-3pm: Occasional gulps of champagne as the team bus heads through the streets of London cheered on by thousands of onlookers. When it finally reaches Trafalgar Square, a hungover Flintoff tells interviewer David Gower: "To be honest with you, David, I'm struggling. I've not been to bed yet. Behind these glasses are a thousand stories."
3pm: The team arrives at 10 Downing Street to be greeted by Prime Minister Tony Blair. Flintoff chills out in a garden deckchair, cool beer in hand.

— MIKE'S MCGRATH PHOBIA —

Former England captain Mike Atherton must have nightmares about Australian fast bowler Glenn McGrath. Between 1995 and 2001 McGrath claimed Atherton's wicket on no fewer than 19 separate occasions – a world Test record for the number of dismissals by a bowler of a particular batsman. Incredibly, on all but one of the 19 times he fell to McGrath, Atherton was caught – usually by wicketkeeper Ian Healy or in the slips.

There was rarely much consolation for Atherton, either, in looking up to the scoreboard as he trudged forlornly off the field. In his innings that were ended by McGrath the England batsman averaged just 9.89 and never once passed 50.

— LILLEE'S HEAVY METAL —

England's 1979/80 tour of Australia was a hastily arranged one during which the Ashes were not at stake. All the same, the First Test in Perth in particular produced some memorable moments.

The fun started on the second morning when Australian tailender Dennis Lillee emerged from the pavilion carrying an aluminium bat manufactured by a friend of his, Graham Monoghan. After Lillee scored three runs from four Ian Botham deliveries, play was stopped following a complaint from England captain Mike Brearley that the metal bat was damaging the ball. A heated ten-minute long discussion between Lillee, Brearley and the umpires ensured before Lillee was eventually persuaded to play on with a conventional wooden bat. Clearly irritated and annoyed, Lillee threw the metal bat away in disgust, earning a warning from the umpires in the process. Lillee had a right to be angry, as there was nothing in the rules to say that he had to use a wooden bat – although this loophole was cleared up some months later.

In the second innings the same player helped produce a few chuckles when he was caught by Peter Willey off the bowling of Graham Dilley. All three players had been around the Test arena for some years but this was the first time that the scorecard read:

'Lillee c Willey b Dilley'.

— CB FRY: THE ULTIMATE ALL-ROUNDER —

CB Fry, who appeared in 18 Ashes Tests between 1899 and 1912, was a sporting phenomenon and a significant figure in the worlds of politics and literature.

One of a select band of double internationals, he won a single cap for England at football against Ireland in 1901. The following year he appeared at full-back in the 1902 FA Cup final for Southampton, having previously played for Oxford University and Corinthians. Fry was also a talented rugby player and athlete, representing Oxford University, Blackheath and the Barbarians in the oval ball game and, in 1883, equalling the world long jump record with a prodigious leap of 23 feet, six and a half inches. Something of a show off, Fry enjoyed demonstrating his athletic prowess at social gatherings, where his party piece was to jump backwards onto a mantelpiece.

But it was at cricket that his sporting ability shone the brightest. A forceful right-hand bat and fast-medium bowler, Fry opened the batting for both Sussex and England, often partnered for both teams by his great friend, the dashing Prince Ranjitsinhji. He first played against the Australians at Trent Bridge in 1899, making a half century after opening the innings with another cricketing legend, WG Grace. Six years later he recorded his highest Test score against the Aussies, hitting 144 at The Oval. This triumph was particularly sweet as the Australians believed that Fry, a fine straight driver, could only score runs in front of the wicket and set their field accordingly. His response, an innings full of fine cuts and delicate glances, showed the error of that assessment. "I had only one stroke; but it went to ten different parts of the field," Fry later joked.

In 1912 Fry captained England in a triangular tournament with Australia and South Africa, remaining undefeated throughout the summer. "He was my skipper and we got on well together," recalled Sir Jack Hobbs of this series. "He was a great raconteur and my wife and I spent many happy hours just listening to him."

Fry continued to live a colourful life in the years after his sporting heyday. He stood unsuccessfully as a Liberal candidate in Sussex, wrote an autobiography and a cricket book entitled *Batsmanship*. He encountered various Prime Ministers from Gladstone to Churchill and, through his friendship with Ranjitsinhji, represented India at the League of Nations. He later flirted with fascism and in 1934 met Hitler, but failed in his efforts to persuade the Nazi regime to take up Test match cricket. Most bizarrely, he was offered the throne of Albania in 1939, but didn't have the necessary £10,000 to accept the post. After suffering a mental breakdown while visiting India, Fry became increasingly eccentric in later life, developing a paranoid fear of Indians and wearing unconventional clothing.

He died at the age of 84 in Hampstead, north London. In his obituary in *The Manchester Guardian*, the cricket writer Neville Cardus wrote: "He was one of the last of the English tradition of the amateur, the connoisseur and, in the most delightful sense of the word, the dilettante."

— SETTLED TEAM —

England used just 12 players during their victorious 2005 Ashes series, and might well have fielded the same starting 11 for all five Tests but for an injury to pace bowler Simon Jones. Yet this model of consistency is not a record for England in Ashes cricket, as during the 1884/85 series in Australia the tourists, led by captain Arthur Shrewsbury, put out the same team in all five Tests.

The same continuity did not extend to their opponents. After losing the First Test, the Australians refused to play in the Second Test in Melbourne unless they were given half the gate money. This demand was rejected, with the result that a completely different Australian side, including nine debutants, took to the field for the match. Faced by what was, in effect, a Second XI, England won comfortably, recording a ten-wicket victory. Flux and change continued to be a theme for the Aussies, who had a different captain for each of the Tests in the five-match series which England won 3–2.

— LONGEST AND SHORTEST MATCHES —

The longest match in Ashes history was way back in 1929, during the era of 'timeless' Tests, and lasted eight days. The close of play scores in the final Test at Melbourne went like this:

Day 1: England 240/4
Day 2: England 485/9
Day 3: England 519, Australia 152/2
Day 4: Australia 367/4
Day 5: Australia 491, England 18/1
Day 6: England 257, Australia 7/0
Day 7: Australia 173/4
Day 8: Australia 287/5 (Australia won by five wickets)

Meanwhile, six Ashes encounters have been settled inside two days, five of them in the nineteenth century when uncovered wickets meant a sudden shower could turn a perfect pitch into an unplayable quagmire in just a few minutes. The only Ashes Test to be finished inside two days in the twentieth century was at Trent Bridge in 1921 when 16 wickets fell on the first day and 14 on the second before Australia ran out winners by ten wickets.

— THE GREAT ASHES SERIES: 'VAUGHAN'S HEROES,' ENGLAND 2005 —

The 2005 Ashes series, between an improving England side under Michael Vaughan and Ricky Ponting's all-conquering Aussies, always promised to be a closely fought contest but nobody could have predicted the heights of excitement this most compelling of duels produced throughout a truly memorable summer.

The First Test at Lord's, however, was disappointingly one-sided. Despite dismissing the Australians cheaply on the first day, England's batsmen were no match for their old bête noire Glenn McGrath and went down to a crushing defeat.

The Aussies' 16-year monopoly of the Ashes looked likely to be extended, but on the morning of the first day's play at the Second Test at Edgbaston the visitors were dealt a significant blow when McGrath stepped on a practice ball, turned his ankle and was declared unfit to play. Despite the loss of his main strike bowler, Ponting elected to field after winning the toss. England's openers, Andrew Strauss and Marcus Trescothick, took full advantage and by the close the home side had rattled up 407 runs. England continued to dictate the game, and by the morning of the fourth day Australia's last two wickets needed to add 107 to prevent the home side levelling the series. The task looked a forlorn one but the tailenders chipped away at the target until, with just three runs required, Steve Harmison sent down a bouncer which flicked Michael Kasprowicz's glove before being snapped up by wicketkeeper Geraint Jones.

England very nearly repeated their dramatic victory in the Third Test at Old Trafford, but were foiled first by Ponting's back-to-the-wall century and then, agonisingly, by a defiant last-wicket stand between McGrath and fellow paceman Brett Lee.

The draw was a disappointment to Vaughan and his men, but they retained the initiative in the Fourth Test at Trent Bridge, forcing Australia to follow on. An easy victory appeared in the bag, but England stumbled in their second innings, only reaching their small target with three wickets in hand.

Still, having fallen behind in the series, Australia now had to win the final Test at The Oval to retain the Ashes. After two roughly equal first innings and numerous interruptions for rain and bad light, everything depended on how England fared on the final day. With Aussie spinner Shane Warne in exceptional form, England were struggling in the early afternoon at 126–5, just 132 runs ahead. But a spectacular innings by Kevin Pietersen, who scored 158 after being dropped twice, ensured that the match would be drawn.

After 16 years of hurt, England had finally won back the Ashes – and, what's more, they had done so in a thrilling style that would be remembered for many summers to come.

First Test: Lord's, July 21–24
Australia 190 & 384, England 155 & 180
Australia won by 239 runs

Second Test: Edgbaston, Aug 4–7
England 407 and 182, Australia 308 & 279
England won by 2 runs

Third Test: Old Trafford, Aug 11–15
England 444 & 280–6 dec, Australia 302 & 371–9
Match drawn

Fourth Test: Trent Bridge, Aug 25–28
England 477 & 129–7 Australia 218 & 387
England won by 3 wickets

Fifth Test: The Oval, Sept 8–12
England 373 & 335, Australia 367 & 4–0
Match drawn

Star performers

For England: Many players chipped in, but all-rounder and national hero Freddie Flintoff was an inspiration.

For Australia: Spinner Shane Warne, who took 40 wickets in the series (becoming the first bowler to pass the 600-mark in Test cricket in the process).

They said it

"Apart from when we won at Lord's, we were never as good as England, and they deserve to win."
Ricky Ponting is magnanimous in defeat

"We had to dig deep on numerous occasions but our team has been fantastic and the way they've risen to the challenge has been incredible."
Michael Vaughan

— THE LONGEST INNINGS —

Unsurprisingly, the highest individual innings in Ashes history, Len Hutton's superb 364 at the Oval in 1938, is also the longest, taking 797 minutes. For Australia, Bobby Simpson holds the record for occupation of the crease, his 311 at Old Trafford in 1964 taking 762 minutes to compile.

— QUIDS IN AT HEADINGLEY —

On the fourth day of the 1981 Test at Headingley everyone in the ground was certain that Australia were not just going to win, but win comfortably. Following on 227 behind, England were reduced to 135–7. The match, as a contest, seemed over. Bookmakers Ladbrokes were certainly of that opinion and, advised by in-house expert Godfrey Evans, a former England wicketkeeper, offered odds of 500–1 on an England victory. Even at those attractive odds there were no takers in the home dressing room: believing that the match would be over by the close of play, the England team had already checked out of their hotel one day early.

What happened next, however, has gone into Ashes folklore. Thanks to a sensational innings of 149 not out by Ian Botham, England recovered to 356 all out, setting Australia 130 to win. Mike Brearley's team then bowled out the visitors for 111 on the final day, with Bob Willis taking eight wickets in an inspired spell of fast bowling.

Incredibly, the Aussies had turned victory into defeat from a near-impregnable position. Understandably, the mood in the away dressing room was sombre, but for a couple of players, fast bowler Dennis Lillee and wicketkeeper Rodney Marsh, there was some consolation. Well aware that strange things can happen in Test cricket, the pair had instructed the team's bus driver, Peter Tribe, to put a few quid on an England victory at the generous odds being offered by Ladbrokes. The Aussies' winnings from their combined stake of £15 amounted to £7,500 – more than enough to buy their dejected team-mates a few consolatory drinks.

— REVEREND LEADS HIS FLOCK —

England's touring party to Australia in 1962/63 included the first ordained minister to play Test cricket, the Reverend David Sheppard.

Sheppard began his Test career in 1950 and, in 1954, captained England in two Tests against Pakistan. Recalled in 1956 towards the end of the Ashes series, he scored a century in the Fourth Test at Old Trafford. Thereafter, his Church of England duties restricted his availability for his county, Sussex, and it appeared that his Test-playing days were over.

However, he was surprisingly recalled once more to the England team in 1962. After performing well against Pakistan, the 33-year-old Sheppard was invited on the following winter's Ashes tour. Taking a sabbatical from his missionary work at the Mayflower Centre in London's East End, Sheppard took the opportunity to preach in

Australian churches as the England team travelled across the country.

If the Reverend ever prayed for good fortune on the cricket field, his calls were answered in the Second Test at Melbourne when he completed his third and final century for England. He was eventually dismissed for 113, run out while attempting to hit the winning single for his team. Nevertheless, England still won the match by seven wickets.

The margin of victory, however, might have been greater if Sheppard had not dropped two catches in the field earlier. One of these gaffes prompted the wisecracking Fred Trueman to quip, "It's a pity Reverend don't put his hands together more often in t'field!"

Sheppard's first-class career ended in 1963, by which point he had accumulated 22 caps. He later became Bishop of Woolwich, before being promoted to the post of Bishop of Liverpool in 1975.

— MEN OF THE MATCH 2010/11 —

Test	Venue	Man of the Match
First	Brisbane	Alastair Cook (Eng)
Second	Adelaide	Kevin Pietersen (Eng)
Third	Perth	Mitchell Johnson (Aus)
Fourth	Melbourne	Jonathan Trott (Eng)
Fifth	Sydney	Alastair Cook (Eng)

In addition to these awards, England opener Alastair Cook was named Man of the Series.

— ASHES LEGENDS: ANDREW FLINTOFF —

Despite making his England debut as far back as 1998, 'Freddie' Flintoff didn't burst into Ashes action until the enthralling 2005 series in England.

The Lancashire all-rounder certainly made up for lost time with some tremendous bravura displays with bat and ball which were instrumental to England's success. In the Second Test at Edgbaston, for example, he tore into the Australian bowling in both innings, his total of nine sixes in the match passing Ian Botham's previous best of six. He also collected seven wickets with his fast, accurate bowling and mastery of reverse swing, leading England captain Michael Vaughan to describe his team's sensational two-run victory as 'Fred's Test'. In England's second win at Trent Bridge Flintoff played one of the crucial innings of the Test, scoring a maiden Ashes century. He finished the summer with a total of 402 Test runs, 24 wickets and was selected as the player of the series by Australian coach, John Buchanan.

Flintoff's spectacular Ashes exploits have since won him a host of other awards, including an MBE, the BBC's 2005 Sports Personality of the Year and the ICC player of the year award, which he shared with South Africa's Jacques Kallis. On England's tour of India in 2006, with Vaughan unavailable through injury, he was promoted to team captain, a position he held for the home series against Sri Lanka.

Flintoff also captained England when they defended the Ashes 'Down Under' in 2006/07. The tour, though, was not a memorable one for the all-rounder who saw his side thrashed 5–0 by a resurgent Australia. Like many of his team-mates, Flintoff failed to reproduce his dynamic form of 2005, recording just two half centuries and taking only 11 wickets in the series. Things got no better for him at the 2007 World Cup in the West Indies, either. After an alcohol-fuelled night out ended with him having to be rescued from a pedalo he had drunkenly taken out into the sea, Flintoff was dropped from the side for the next match and unceremoniously stripped of the vice-captaincy.

Freddie Flintoff

Sadly, he was plagued by injury in the ensuing seasons and during the 2009 Ashes series announced his retirement from Test cricket at the end of the summer. Typically, though, he went out on a high, earning the Man of the Match award for his performance in the Lord's Test as England beat the Aussies at the home of cricket for the first time in 75 years and playing a full part in his side's eventual 2–1 series triumph.

Since retiring from all forms of cricket in 2010, Flintoff has forged a successful career in the media, notably as a team captain in the sports panel show *A League of their Own*.

Andrew Flintoff factfile
Born: Preston, 6 December 1977
County: Lancashire
Ashes Tests: 14 (2005–09)
Batting: 856 runs (ave 34.24)
Bowling: 43 wickets (ave 36.12)

Others on Flintoff

"Flintoff is the superstar and definitely the difference between the sides in this series. He has dragged us back into matches on so many occasions."
Geoffrey Boycott, after England's Ashes victory, September 2005

"Flintoff is the best in the world at the moment. Any captain would want him in the team."
Australian wicketkeeper **Adam Gilchrist**, September 2005

— FASTEST AND SLOWEST CENTURIONS —

Australian wicketkeeper Adam Gilchrist struck the fastest century in Ashes history in the Third Test of the 2006/07 series at Perth, reaching three figures off just 57 balls. His extraordinary hundred took only one ball more than the fastest ever Test match ton, by West Indies legend Viv Richards against England at St John's, Antigua in 1986. Gilchrist's quickfire knock included 12 fours, four sixes and 24 runs taken off a single Monty Panesar over (026646), the most runs conceded by a bowler in an Ashes over.

Before that dramatic innings by Gilchrist, the record for the fastest hundred in Ashes Tests was held by Gilbert Jessop, one of the most fabled all-rounders in English cricket history. At The Oval in 1902, Jessop, dubbed 'The Croucher' for his trademark squat stance, smacked his ton in just 75 minutes, taking only 76 balls to reach three figures.

Clearly, one spectator at least was expecting something special when Jessop marched to the wicket, as he decided to make a ball-by-ball record of the batsman's innings – one of the earliest instances of this aspect of the scorer's art. Jessop's whirlwind innings was the turning point of the match as England, chasing 263 to win, recovered from 48–5 to triumph by one wicket. The Gloucestershire batsman's blistering assault on the Aussies was not untypical, his aggressive approach once leading CB Fry to comment: "No man has ever driven the ball so hard, so high and so often in so many different directions."

The fastest double and treble Ashes centuries were both notched by Don Bradman in his famous innings of 334 at Headingley in 1930. The Aussie maestro took just 214 minutes to hit 200 and 336 minutes to reach 300.

England opener Mike Atherton holds the record for the slowest Ashes hundred, taking 424 minutes and 326 balls to make a ton at Sydney in 1991. Yet Atherton's innings was almost Jessop-like compared to the snoozathon England's Trevor Bailey subjected the Brisbane crowd to in 1958. With the visitors fighting a grim rearguard action, Bailey took 357 minutes and 350 balls to reach 50. Much to the relief of the home crowd – or at least those who hadn't nodded off to sleep – Bailey was eventually out for 68 and Australia went on to win the match.

– YORKSHIRE'S FINEST –

A total of 433 players have represented England in Ashes matches, and proud Yorkshiremen (and women) will be delighted to discover that the white rose county leads the way when it comes to providing cricketers for the national team. According to research carried out by Malcolm Ashton, a former England scorer who is now the *Test Match Special* statistician, the counties with the most players to have taken part in the Ashes are:

County	Ashes players
Yorkshire	59
Middlesex	47
Surrey	45
Lancashire	44
Kent	41

— ASHES 2005: A SUMMER TO REMEMBER —

A selection of quotes from the greatest England-Australia series ever:

"If any of our batsmen get out to Ashley Giles in the Tests they should go and hang themselves."
Former Australian bowler **Terry Alderman** before the start of the series. Giles ended up taking 10 wickets

"Hoggard's like a net bowler when you compare him to McGrath and Kasprowicz."
Former Aussie bowler **Jeff Thomson** prior to the start of the 2005 series. Hoggard answered the criticism by taking 18 wickets

"We have put ourselves in a position of real strength and can push on to fulfill our goal of winning this series 5–0."
Matthew Hayden gets carried away after Australia's victory in the First Test

"The task is formidable and nobody has ever shied away from that fact. My prediction is 2–1 to England, so I'm still on course for that."
David Graveney, chairman of England selectors, displays his Mystic Meg-like powers after defeat in the First Test at Lord's

"It's been an epic game. I think most of my guys thought that it had gone but we fought hard."
Michael Vaughan, after England's two-run victory in the Second Test at Edgbaston

"Oh dear, the riff-raff who have started to clamber on the bandwagon. They are talking about Freddie and Tres and Hoggy as if they have known them all their lives . . . They have obviously decided that cricket is the new sex and want a piece of the action before the next new sex comes along."
Max Davidson, *The Daily Telegraph*

"You can never think you've done it against Australia."
Michael Vaughan, after the Aussies' last wicket pair held out for a draw at Old Trafford

"Bizarrely, I was very confident."
Matthew Hoggard, after his innings of eight not out helped England creep home in the Fourth Test at Trent Bridge

"It was real grandchildren stuff. 'Gather round and I'll tell you about that innings I played with Pietersen, with the white stripes and the earrings.'"
Ashley Giles, on his Ashes-winning innings at The Oval

"Nothing I did that day was more important than us winning the Ashes. It was all about us winning the Ashes."
Kevin Pietersen on the same innings

"A fellow sporting £50,000-worth of diamond ear studs and apparently wearing a dead skunk under his helmet enabled England to tear the Ashes from Australia's grasp."
The Guardian hails Ashes hero Kevin Pietersen

"I just thought, well, they're only out on loan, the Ashes. It's less than 18 months away, and then we'll have them back."
Ricky Ponting, looking on the positive side at The Oval

"This was the England cricket team, for heaven's sake, being greeted on the streets of London as though they were pioneering astronauts getting a tickertape reception through New York."
Wisden editor **Matthew Engel** on the Ashes victory celebrations

"Crowd estimates are invariably as trustworthy as a dodgy builder's, but there were decidedly more than the two men and a dog Matthew Hoggard said he was expecting."
Stephen Brenkley, Wisden 2005

"Elton John played a big part in our Ashes win because *Rocket Man* was our anthem."
Andrew Flintoff, April 2006

— ASHES 2006/07: A WINTER TO FORGET —

A selection of quotes following Australia's 5–0 whitewash:

"Lots of so-called experts said England would win . . . so it's a great feeling right at the moment."
Australia captain **Ricky Ponting**, enjoying his side's victory

"Australia have raised the bar in this series. They've just been awesome . . . they really made it tough for us."
England captain **Andrew Flintoff** accepts his team were second-best

"To win 5–0 and finish on such a high was just fantastic."
Shane Warne, confirming that this would be his last Test series

"This has to be the biggest wake-up call in English cricket, and if attention is paid to this thrashing, then something good will come from it."
BBC commentator **Jonathan Agnew** tries to look on the bright side

— BAT AND BALL XI —

A team of Ashes cricketers who were also pretty useful at football:

1. CB Fry (1899–1912), one England football cap
2. Billy Gunn (1887–99), two England football caps
3. Denis Compton (1938–56), Arsenal and 12 wartime England football caps
4. 'Tip' Foster (1903–04), five England football caps
5. Willie Watson (1953–59), four England football caps
6. Ian Botham (1977–89), Scunthorpe United
7. Arthur Milton (1958–59), one England football cap
8. Alfred Lyttleton (1880–84), one England football cap
9. Harry Makepeace (1920–21), four England football caps
10. Arnie Sidebottom (1985), Manchester United
11. Leslie Gay (1894), two England football caps

— THE STRANGE CASE OF BILLY MIDWINTER —

Medium pacer Billy Midwinter is the only cricketer to have played both for and against England in Tests with Australia.

Born in St Briavels, Gloucestershire in 1851, Midwinter emigrated with his parents to Australia aged nine. A talented all-rounder, he made his debut for the Aussies in the first England-Australia clash in 1877. Later that year he returned to England to play for WG Grace's Gloucestershire – becoming, in effect, the first overseas professional to appear in the English game – and he continued to turn out for the county until 1882. However, after playing four Tests for England on the tour of Australia in 1881/82, he emigrated Down Under for a second time. In 1884, while playing state cricket for Victoria, he was selected for the Australians' tour of England, wearing the baggy green cap in all three Tests. His return to the Aussie fold makes Midwinter the only cricketer to have played for one country, then another, and then a second time for his original international team.

Apart from Midwinter, four other nineteenth-century cricketers – Billy Murdoch, John Ferris, Sammy Woods and Albert Trott – played for both Australia and England, although none of this quartet appeared for both countries in Ashes matches.

— AUSSIES DRAW A BLANK —

You have to go back to 1977 for the last time that Australia failed to win a single Test in an Ashes series, home nation England wining three and drawing two of the five encounters between the sides.

England's hopes were raised when Australia arrived in the northern hemisphere without their star bowler Dennis Lillee, who was suffering from a back injury. The tourists were also hampered by divisions in their camp between the majority of their number, who had committed themselves to joining Kerry Packer's rebel World Series Cricket after the tour, and the remaining players and management who had promised to stay loyal to the Australian Cricket Board. For their part, England were not unaffected by the 'Packer Circus', as it was dubbed by its many critics, skipper Tony Greig losing the captaincy to Mike Brearley when it became known that he had signed up for the breakaway enterprise. However, to the annoyance of many England supporters who made their feelings clear throughout the summer, Greig's usefulness as an all-rounder meant that he retained his place in the side.

Following a draw in the first Test at Lord's, England took full advantage of the tourists' lack of unity to win by nine wickets at Old Trafford, thanks in part to a century by Bob Woolmer and a six-wicket haul for spinner Derek Underwood in the Aussie's second innings.

Ending his three-year self-imposed exile from Test cricket, legendary batsman Geoff Boycott returned to the England fold amid much fanfare for the Third Test at Trent Bridge. To no great surprise, he made an immediate impact by notching a century – but not before he had incurred the displeasure of the home crowd by inadvertently running out local hero Derek Randall. Set under 200 to win in their second innings, England made their target with some ease after Boycott and Brearley put on an impressive 154 for the first wicket.

Boycott was again the headline performer in the Fourth Test, hitting a superb 191 on his home ground of Headingley to record his hundredth hundred in first-class cricket. Blown away for just 103 in their first innings (a young Ian Botham taking 5-21), the Aussies fared little better when they followed on and were beaten by an innings and 83 runs.

With the Ashes lost, the Baggy Greens only had pride to play for in the final Test at The Oval. However, their chances of claiming a consolation victory were all but ended when the first day's play was washed out and, despite taking a first innings lead of 171 runs, the visitors had to be satisfied with a draw.

Since 1977 England and Australia have met in 17 Ashes series in which the Aussies have always won at least one Test. England, on the other hand, have failed to secure even a single victory on four occasions – in 1979/80, 1989, 1990/91 and, most recently, in 2006/07.

— THE GREAT ASHES SERIES: 'ENGLAND'S CRUSHING VICTORY', AUSTRALIA 2010/11 —

After regaining the Ashes on home turf in 2009, England travelled to Australia in buoyant mood and keen to gain revenge for the 5–0 humiliation they had suffered on their last trip Down Under three years earlier.

Andrew Strauss's men, though, got off to a poor start in the First Test in Brisbane, posting a disappointing score on a good pitch, Aussie quick Peter Siddle doing the damage with six wickets, including a hat-trick. The hosts replied with 481, Mike Hussey (195) and wicketkeeper Brad Haddin (136) both notching centuries in a huge sixth-wicket stand, to put Australia in the driving seat. To the delight of the Barmy Army, however, England's top order displayed grit and determination on an epic scale in their second innings, Strauss (110), Alastair Cook (235 not out) and Jonathan Trott (135 not out) all passing three figures as the visitors battered the Aussies into the ground before declaring on 517–1, the draw safely achieved.

England's domination of the Australian bowlers continued at Adelaide, with Cook (148) and Kevin Pietersen (227) starring as the tourists claimed a massive first innings lead. The deficit proved too great for the hosts to claw back and, thanks in part to a five-wicket haul by spinner Graeme Swann, England secured an innings victory inside four days.

Down but not out, Australia fought back in the Third Test at Perth, fast bowler Mitchell Johnson taking 6–38 on a pacy wicket to leave England trailing. Sensing their chance, the home side rammed home their advantage in the second innings, Mike Hussey making a century to set the visitors nearly 400 to win. For the only time in the series England failed to rise to the occasion, Aussie quick Ryan Harris claiming six wickets as the hosts levelled the series with a day to spare.

Other England sides might have crumbled after that setback, but not this one. Instead, the tourists blitzed out the Aussies for just 98 at Melbourne, Jimmy Anderson and Chris Tremlett taking four wickets each in front of a stunned Boxing Day home crowd. Building on this flying start, England rubbed the Aussie bowlers' faces in the dirt, Trott leading the way with a magnificent 168 as the visitors passed the 500-mark for the third time. Tim Bresnan then took four wickets as the Aussies were again dismissed cheaply, to give England victory by the massive margin of an innings and 157 runs.

With the Ashes in the bag, England could have been forgiven for relaxing in the final Test at Sydney. However, Strauss and co. were eager to finish the tour on a high and, after bowling out the Baggy

Greens for under 300 for the fifth time in the series, Cook (189), Ian Bell (115) and wicketkeeper Matt Prior (118) all made centuries as the tourists posted another mammoth total. Predictably, the by now shell-shocked Aussies provided little resistance second time round, succumbing to a third innings defeat – the first time in the history of Test cricket that the hosts had suffered a trio of such stuffings.

For England, on the other hand, the tour could hardly have gone better, and their 3–1 triumph was just reward for a magnificent team effort.

First Test: Brisbane, Nov 25–29
England 260 & 517/1dec, Australia 481 & 107/1
Match drawn

Second Test: Adelaide, Dec 3–7
Australia 245 & 304, England 620/5 dec
England won by an innings and 71 runs

Third Test: Perth, Dec 16–19
Australia 268 & 309, England 187 & 123
Australia won by 267 runs

Fourth Test: Melbourne, Dec 26–29
Australia 98 & 258, England 513
England won by an innings and 157 runs

Fifth Test: Sydney, Jan 3–7
Australia 280 & 281, England 644
England won by an innings and 83 runs

Star performers

For Australia: Mike Hussey was the one Australian batsman to impose himself on the English bowlers, scoring two centuries and compiling 570 runs in total.

For England: Opener Alastair Cook's 766 runs (at an incredible average of 127.67) provided the bedrock for his team's triumph, while Jimmy Anderson was the pick of the bowlers with 24 wickets (average 26.04).

They said it

"We played three outstanding Test matches and to win the Ashes here in style will be something that will live long in my memory."
Andrew Strauss

"They certainly deserve it – they outplayed us in every facet of the game, they even caught as well as I've seen any team catch."
Michael Clarke, Australia's captain in the final Test

— ASHES 2010/11: GOLDEN MEMORIES —

A round-up of the best quotes following England's stunning success Down Under:

"Retaining the Ashes was a fantastic achievement, but winning the series really is the icing on the cake."
Prime Minister **David Cameron** falls back on a well-worn cliché while offering his congratulations to the victorious England team.

"It's been an amazing series for me. I couldn't have imagined this seven weeks ago, so I'm delighted."
England batting hero **Alastair Cook**.

"To bow out in front of so many English fans, having won the Ashes in Australia, it couldn't get any better."
England's **Paul Collingwood**, after announcing his retirement from Test cricket.

"Australia only scored 400 once in the series. Not one of their top four batsmen scored a century, the first time that has happened since 1956. They've been outclassed."
Former England captain **Michael Vaughan**, revelling in some of the key stats from the series.

"It was such slow, painful torture that you wondered whether this is what it must be like to be squeezed to death by a boa constrictor."
Melbourne newspaper *The Herald Sun* sees something snake-like in England's triumph.

The Sprinkler Dance

"The bowlers were fantastic, and the batsmen dipped their bread in it again. We're certainly going to enjoy this."
Andrew Strauss, after England's victory at Sydney in the Fifth Test wrapped up a 3–1 series win.

"I thought the presentation was awful. Forget Cooky's medal, no champagne, no individual medals. The boys deserved better than that! Disgraceful!"
Former England skipper **Andrew Flintoff** laments the lack of booze at the presentation ceremony after the final Test.

"The way things are going, the next Ashes series cannot come too quickly for England. What a shame that we have to wait until 2013 to play this lot again."
England legend **Geoff Boycott**.

— FANS COME TO ENGLAND'S AID —

By the time of the fifth and final Test at The Oval in 1968, Australia were 1–0 up and certain of holding on to the Ashes. However, Colin Cowdrey's England were determined to level the series, and that's precisely what they were on the verge of doing until the weather intervened.

Set 352 to win, Australia were struggling on 86–5 at lunch when a violent thunderstorm flooded almost the entire playing area. The match looked likely to be abandoned as a draw, the prospects for any play at all seeming bleak even after the storm ended and the sun came out. England's one hope lay with the Surrey groundstaff who began an epic mopping-up exercise, assisted by dozens of volunteers from the crowd. Carrying brooms and blankets, they waded through the huge puddles covering the outfield, and vigorously brushed the surface water towards the boundary edge before laying the blankets on the sodden turf.

Finally, with 75 minutes remaining, play was able to resume with sawdust covering the pitch surrounds. For over half an hour the efforts of the fans appeared futile as the Australian sixth-wicket pair of John Inverarity and wicketkeeper Barry Jarman provided dogged resistance. But finally, after Basil D'Oliveira made the breakthrough by bowling Jarman, Australia collapsed. England's hero was left-arm spinner Derek 'Deadly' Underwood, who ripped through the tail to finish with figures of 7–50. Mind you, it was a close run thing. When Underwood trapped Inverarity lbw to seal England's victory by 226 runs only five minutes were left on the clock. As it turned out, the fans who had worked tirelessly in the outfield had been just as crucial to the home team's triumph as the eleven players on the pitch.

— COLLY'S DOUBLE TON IN VAIN —

England's 2006/07 Ashes tour Down Under provided a bare minimum of highlights, but more than a few glasses would have been raised to Paul Collingwood during the Second Test in Adelaide when the all-rounder became the first Englishman since Wally Hammond in 1929 to score a double century against the Aussies on their home patch. Unfortunately, Colly's superb first innings 206 was not enough to prevent England going down to eventual defeat by six wickets, but it did grab him a place in the record books for the highest score by a batsman on the losing side in an Ashes test.

Incidentally, just one other player has passed the 200 mark in an Ashes test and still ended up on the losing team. That was Syd Gregory in the First Test at Sydney in 1894, who made 201 for Australia but then watched in amazement as England went on to win by 10 runs despite following on 251 runs in arrears after their first innings.

— THE DON'S FIRST BAT GOES UNDER THE HAMMER —

In 2006 the bat used by Sir Donald Bradman in his Test debut against England at Brisbane in 1928 was sold to an undisclosed buyer for Aus$58,000. Surprisingly, given his later success, Bradman had a poor debut, scoring just 18 and 1 as England cruised to an innings victory. The young batsman was dropped for the next match, but was recalled for the Third Test at Melbourne where he scored the first of his 29 Test centuries for Australia.

— ENGLAND V AUSTRALIA: THE COMPLETE RECORD —

Year	Venue	Tests	Eng	Aus	Draws	Ashes held by
1877*	Australia	2	1	1	0	-
1879*	Australia	1	0	1	0	-
1880*	England	1	1	0	0	-
1881/82*	Australia	4	0	2	2	-
1882*	England	1	0	1	0	-
1882/83^	Australia	4	2	2	0	England
1884	England	3	1	0	2	England
1884/85	Australia	5	3	2	0	England
1886	England	3	3	0	0	England
1887	Australia	2	2	0	0	England

1888	Australia	1	1	0	0	England
1888	England	3	2	1	0	England
1890+	England	2	2	0	0	England
1892	Australia	3	1	2	0	Australia
1893	England	3	1	0	2	England
1894/95	Australia	5	3	2	0	England
1896	England	3	2	1	0	England
1897/98	Australia	5	1	4	0	Australia
1899	England	5	0	1	4	Australia
1901/02	Australia	5	1	4	0	Australia
1902	England	5	1	2	2	Australia
1903/04	Australia	5	3	2	0	England
1905	England	5	2	0	3	England
1907/08	Australia	5	1	4	0	Australia
1909	England	5	1	2	2	Australia
1911/12	Australia	5	4	1	0	England
1912	England	3	1	0	2	England
1920/21	Australia	5	0	5	0	Australia
1921	England	3	0	3	0	Australia
1924/25	Australia	5	1	4	0	Australia
1926	England	5	1	0	4	England
1928/29	Australia	5	4	1	0	England
1930	England	5	1	2	2	Australia
1932/33	Australia	5	4	1	0	England
1934	England	5	1	2	2	Australia
1936/37	Australia	5	2	3	0	Australia
1938+	England	4	1	1	2	Australia
1946/47	Australia	5	0	3	2	Australia
1948	England	5	0	4	1	Australia
1950/51	Australia	5	1	4	0	Australia
1953	England	5	1	0	4	England
1954/55	Australia	5	3	1	1	England
1956	England	5	2	1	2	England
1958/59	Australia	5	0	4	1	Australia
1961	England	5	1	2	2	Australia
1962/63	Australia	5	1	1	3	Australia
1964	England	5	0	1	4	Australia
1965/66	Australia	5	1	1	3	Australia
1968	England	5	1	1	3	Australia
1970/71+	Australia	6	2	0	4	England
1972	England	5	2	2	1	England
1974/75	Australia	6	1	4	1	Australia
1975	England	4	0	1	3	Australia

1977*	Australia	1	0	1	0	-
1977	England	5	3	0	2	England
1978/79	Australia	6	5	1	0	England
1979/80*	Australia	3	0	3	0	-
1980*	England	1	0	0	1	-
1981	England	6	3	1	2	England
1982/83	Australia	5	1	2	2	Australia
1985	England	6	3	1	2	England
1986/87	Australia	5	2	1	2	England
1988*	Australia	1	0	0	1	-
1989	England	6	0	4	2	Australia
1990/91	Australia	5	0	3	2	Australia
1993	England	6	1	4	1	Australia
1994/95	Australia	5	1	3	1	Australia
1997	England	6	2	3	1	Australia
1998/99	Australia	5	1	3	1	Australia
2001	England	5	1	4	0	Australia
2002/03	Australia	5	1	4	0	Australia
2005	England	5	2	1	2	England
2006/07	Australia	5	0	5	0	Australia
2009	England	5	2	1	2	England
2010/11	Australia	5	3	1	1	England

* Ashes not contested

^ England won the Ashes 2–1, after which an extra game was played which Australia won

+ One Test abandoned without a ball being bowled

— BIBLIOGRAPHY —

Jonathan Agnew with Nick Constable, *Aggers' Special Delivery: Trivial Delights from the World of Cricket* (Sanctuary Publishing Limited, 2005)

John Arlott, *Australian Test Journal* (Sportsmans Book Club, 1956)

Mike Atherton, *Opening Up: My Autobiography* (Hodder & Stoughton Ltd, 2002)

Mark Baldwin, *The Ashes' Strangest Moments* (Robson Books, 2005)

Richie Benaud, *Anything but an Autobiography* (Hodder & Stoughton Ltd, 1998)

Richie Benaud, *My Spin on Cricket* (Hodder & Stoughton Ltd, 2005)

Ian Botham, *Botham: My Autobiography: Don't Tell Kath* (CollinsWillow, 1994)

Ian Botham, *My Autobiography* (HarperCollinsWillow, 2000)

Matthew Engel (ed), *Wisden Cricketers' Almanack 2006* (John Wisden and Co. Ltd, 2006)

Keith Fletcher, *Ashes to Ashes* (Headline Book Publishing Ltd, 2005)

David Hopps, *Great Cricket Quotes* (Robson Books, 1998)

Nasser Hussain, *Playing With Fire: The Autobiography* (Michael Joseph Ltd, 2004)

Douglas Jardine, *Quest for the Ashes* (Hutchinson and co. 1933)

Justin Langer and Steve Harmison: *Ashes Diaries* (Green Umbrella Publishing, 2007)

Dennis Lillee, *Menace: The Autobiography* (Headline Book Publishing Ltd, 2003)

David Norrie, *The Oval Reflections* (Vision Sports Publishing, 2005)

Alec Stewart, *Playing For Keeps* (BBC Books, 2003)

Shane Warne, *My Autobiography* (Hodder & Stoughton Ltd, 2001)

Steve Waugh, *Out of My Comfort Zone: The Autobiography* (Michael Joseph Ltd, 2006)

Bernard Wimpress and Nigel Hart, *Great Ashes Battles* (Andre Deutsch, 1995)